Entrepreneur® MAGAZINE'S

startup

Start Your Own

BUSINESS ON eBAY

Your Step-by-Step Guide to Success

Jacquelyn Lynn

Ep
Entrepreneur.
Press

Editorial Director: Jere L. Calmes
Managing Editor: Marla Markman
Cover Design: Beth Hansen-Winter
Production: Eliot House Productions
Composition: Ed Stevens

This publication is designed to provide accurate and authoritative information in regard to
the subject matter covered. It is sold with the understanding that the publisher is not
engaged in rendering legal, accounting, or other professional services. If legal advice or
other expert assistance is required, the services of a competent professional person should be
sought.

Library of Congress Cataloging-in-Publication Data
Lynn, Jacquelyn.
    Entrepreneur magazine's start your own business on eBAY/by Jacquelyn Lynn.
      p.   cm.
    Includes bibliographical references and index.
    ISBN 1-932531-12-2
      1. Internet auctions. 2. eBay (Firm) 3. Electronic commerce—Management.
4. New business enterprises—Management. 5. Small business—Management.
I. Title: Start your own business on eBAY. II. Entrepreneur (Irvine, Calif.) III. Title.

HF5478.L96 2004
658.8'7—dc22   2004046941

Printed in Canada

10 09 08 07 06 05 04   10 9 8 7 6 5 4 3 2 1

Contents

▲

▲

Preface

It's one of those business success stories that has already become a legend in its own time: eBay, the hottest way to buy and sell goods and services over the Internet.

Online auctions in general and eBay in particular are changing the way merchandise is bought and sold all over the world. They've made it easier than ever for people to start retail businesses and for existing businesses to expand to a worldwide market.

When we say, "start an eBay business," what we really mean is to start a business that uses eBay as a marketing and distribution tool, or to add this element to an existing operation. You're not starting an "eBay business"; you're starting a business selling whatever products you've decided to sell on eBay. This book is not about how to start an online auction business; it's about how to use online auctions, eBay in particular, to start and grow your own business.

Are you a little uncomfortable with the idea of doing business in the vast world of cyberspace? Don't be. E-commerce is finally finding its place in the business world. The spectacular rise and equally spectacular crash of the dotcoms during the '90s was just part of the process of learning how to best use the Internet. What happened in the dotcom debacle is not unique in business. It's happened in other industries at other points in history. People get excited and for some reason decide that the basic fundamentals of doing business don't apply to them. And they fail.

If you're excited about doing business on eBay, that's great. You should be. Just don't get so excited that you do stupid things. If you start to run your company using sound business principles, you'll succeed.

Keep in mind that many of the dotcom companies that were formed in the 1990s are still thriving. Why? Because they have products people want to buy, they have a clear plan, and they use sound business management techniques. If you choose your products carefully, develop a plan and manage your operation well, your company will join the ranks of successful e-commerce operations. This book will help you do that, but it won't do the work for you, and it won't tell you how to make jillions of dollars working just two hours a week. What it will do is serve as a guide, a roadmap for you to use in getting your company launched. Like most businesses, operating on eBay will offer rewards proportionate to your efforts. With your own plan, a system, and the perseverance to follow it through, you can enjoy consistent profits from your eBay activities.

A lot of companies out there offer plans and systems to help people get started in an online business. Some are legitimate, but too many are scams that will just cost you money. And some of the legitimate operators sell the same advice to all their clients, which means you risk ending up with a cookie-cutter operation that has the same look and same products as hundreds of other sites, with lots of competition and few, if any, customers. Nothing can take the place of doing your own research and preparation, and putting the stamp of your own personality on your business.

Maybe, like many of the eBay sellers we talked with, you're a shopper who needs to make money to continue to buy. Or like one seller, you've bought too much and want to get rid of that stuff. Or like all the sellers we talked with, you have an entrepreneurial spirit, you want to start your own business, and eBay is an appropriate sales vehicle.

Whatever is motivating you, know this: Doing business on eBay is fun, exciting, profitable—and hard work. If you're not willing to put in the effort and the hours, no amount of information will make you successful.

Regardless of the particular type of business you want to own, how much money you have, whether you want to be homebased or operate from a commercial location, this book will tell you how to use eBay to start and grow. We'll begin with an overview of online auctions, look at the products and services you can sell, and then go through the step-by-step process of setting up and running your new venture. Throughout the book, you'll hear from successful eBay sellers who have built profitable operations and are eager to share what they've learned in the process. Of course, reading a book can only take you so far; once you actually start selling on eBay, you'll work and learn as you go.

Whether you plan to start a part-time business by yourself or jump into eBay selling full time and hire employees, we recommend you read every chapter in this book because most of the information applies to all sizes and types of eBay operations, and the information is interrelated.

So relax and start reading. The thrilling and lucrative world of selling on eBay is within your reach.

Introduction
to eBay

The goal of this book is to teach you how to build a profitable business selling on eBay—and the most important word in this sentence is *profitable*. Making sales on eBay is simple, and you can learn how to do that by just browsing the site. But if you're serious about your business, then the point of selling on eBay is to make a profit.

Beware!
EBay transactions are between the buyer and seller. As the online auction site, eBay is merely the vehicle that brings the buyer and seller together. EBay will assist with disputes but is not ultimately responsible for the transaction.

Before we get into the nuts and bolts of successful eBay selling, let's take a look at how this opportunity came to be.

The first online auction venue hit the Internet in 1994. The following year, Pierre Omidyar introduced the site that would eventually be known as eBay. Originally called Auction Web, it started out as a kind of virtual garage sale, but with the added excitement of auction pricing. And it was so successful that it didn't take long for other online auction sites to pop up.

The big advantage of online auctions is that they expand a seller's market from a relatively small local group to essentially anyone with a computer and access to the Internet. And it didn't take long for major companies, both business-to-consumer and business-to-business, to realize that this was a sales opportunity they couldn't afford to overlook.

What this means for you as an eBay seller is that you've stepped onto a level playing field that's populated with sellers that range from small part-timers who may not post even an auction a month to huge multinational corporations with hundreds of items up for sale at any given time. And your chances of profits and success are just as good as theirs.

If you want to sell merchandise to consumers, eBay is a great way to do that without having to deal with the overhead expense of having a retail store. If you already have a retail operation, eBay opens up a tremendous market for you at virtually no additional cost. Millions of dollars are spent and earned on eBay every day. If you want to sell merchandise or services of any kind, you can't afford to overlook this sales channel.

According to its corporate mission statement, eBay's mission is "to provide a global trading platform where practically anyone can trade practically anything." The site has more than 61 million registered users worldwide who trade goods and services in about 18,000 categories. On any given day, there are some 12 million items for sale on eBay, generating about $40 million in sales. That means that annual sales transacted on eBay total nearly $15 billion and growing.

And yet, according to eBay spokesperson Kevin Pursglove, eBay has penetrated only a very small percentage—perhaps 4 percent or less—of its potential market. That means the time is right for you to start selling on eBay.

Like Eating a Good Breakfast

You know how important it is to start the day right with a good breakfast, don't you? The same principle applies to selling on eBay: Get started right, and the path to profits will be much easier to navigate.

Paul Mladjenovic, a small-business specialist who also teaches classes on Internet auctions, says many eBay sellers fail because they jump in without adequate research and preparation. "There are people who say, 'Why don't I just give it a shot?' and they list something. Then it doesn't work out and the listing closes without selling, and they think this is not for them," he says. In reality, many of these people could have been very successful had they taken the time to learn how to sell through online auctions before putting up their first listing.

While it is true that you learn by doing—as all the eBay sellers we spoke with agree—there are a few things you should learn *before* doing. After all, there's no reason for you to repeat the mistakes of others. Of course, if you already have, that's OK. Among its many benefits is the fact that eBay is a very forgiving business venue. No, there aren't any "do-overs," but there are plenty of chances to do it again—the right way.

On these pages, you're going to meet a number of successful eBay sellers, and they've all made plenty of mistakes. More important, though, is that they all do a lot of things very right—which translates into very profitable businesses.

Who Are the eBay Sellers?

Successful eBay sellers come from all backgrounds, with an infinite range of experience and goals. Jonathan Garriss and David Topkins were working on Wall Street—Garriss as a portfolio manager and Topkins as a syndicate manager—when they started selling on eBay. It wasn't something they deliberately set out to do. Topkins' parents were moving out of the home he grew up in, and neither they nor he had room to store his childhood collectibles, such as baseball cards. "He didn't want to just throw them out, so he had to do something," recalls Garriss. "So we started selling them on eBay, and it was very successful. Word got around, and all of a sudden, everybody we knew who wanted to clear out their closets was coming to us to sell the stuff for them."

The pair got involved with some charities, selling items on eBay to help raise funds for worthy causes. It didn't take these two young hotshot Wall Street guys long to realize they had found an opportunity that would not only be lucrative, but also give them the sense of personal satisfaction they were missing. "Don't get me wrong—the money is great on Wall Street," Garriss says. "But there are other things you need. And this took off on its own and dragged us along with it."

Garriss and Topkins formed Gotham City Online in New York City and started selling on eBay part time in January 1999; Garriss left Wall Street to focus full time on the eBay selling operation in October of the same year, and Topkins followed in January 2000. Today, with a product line focusing on clothing and accessories, Gotham City Online's sales exceed $1 million annually and are doubling every six months.

Adam Ginsberg spent 11 years in direct sales before opening his own company selling home furnishings and pool tables through a traditional wholesale/retail outlet format. In October 2001, he put a pool table up for auction on eBay "for fun." It sold at a good price, so he put another one up. By the following summer, he was selling 25 tables a week on eBay. "The average pool table store in the United States sells three to four [tables] a week," Ginsberg says. Even so, he adds, "I wasn't taking eBay that seriously. I had my retail location in Los Angeles." But he concedes that he didn't particularly enjoy going to that store every day; rather, he much preferred staying home, working on his computer. He opened an eBay store and watched his sales continue to climb. A year after that first eBay sale, ZBilliards was selling 150 to 175 pool tables a week on eBay—that's about $15 million a year in revenue—and Ginsberg finally shut down his retail outlet.

Ginsberg has since opened a second eBay store, ZBilliard Corner, to sell pool table accessories, and a third store that sells home furnishings—and he's still working from home, although now he shares his basement office with three staffers. "I'm not through yet," he says. "I see all these vertical markets, related or unrelated to each other, where we can utilize the same philosophy and strategy that we have created to sell our pool tables."

David Schultz's path to eBay sales was more purposeful. He was working for a children's furniture company and given the task of finding ways the company could sell on the Internet. He did the job so well that he eventually left that company and, with partner Matt Brannon, formed IEP Visions, an Orlando, Florida-based company that sells children's furniture online. About 90 to 95 percent of his sales (at $2 million-plus annually and growing) are on eBay.

Not all successful eBay sellers fall into such high-volume operations. Sue Rudolph is a semiretired antiques dealer in Winter Park, Florida, who started selling on eBay after she closed her retail shop. "I have, as most antiques dealers do, a lot of things that have worth," says the owner of Sweet Sue's Antiques and Appraisals. "I thought it would be nice to sell some of those things and have a little extra income."

She says eBay and other online auctions have had a tremendous impact on how antiques and collectibles dealers run their businesses. When her shop was open, she considered it a good week if 100 prospective customers came through the door, and she routinely had to deal with face-to-face buyers trying to negotiate for lower prices. By contrast, she points out, on eBay, millions of potential customers are online every day, driving prices up with their bids, competing for the opportunity to buy your merchandise.

Linda Parker is a stay-at-home mom in Tustin, California, who sells part time on eBay. She specializes in glassware and china, but also sells collectibles and random off-beat items. "I discovered eBay as a buyer," she says. "I began selling because I realized that if I was bidding more than I should on things, other people were, too. And I had a lot of things around the house that I wanted to get rid of but didn't think I could get much for them at a garage sale. For example, I had a Winnie the Pooh switch plate that I would have been lucky to get $2 for at a garage sale, but I sold it on eBay for $12." Her eBay activities are turning into a family business: Her nine-year-old son has been known to go

> ## Fun Fact
> Many successful eBay sellers got their start as a lark, posting an auction just to see what would happen, or selling a few things to make money to pay for the things they wanted to buy.

through his room looking for items to sell, and her husband has even sold a few things. She predicts her two-year-old son will follow in their footsteps.

Since she began selling on eBay in 2000, Laurie Ayers says her income has doubled every year, and she is able to be home with her daughter. She sells some new items, but mostly "gently used" things she finds at thrift stores and garage sales. Like so many eBay sellers, the single mom in Granville, Michigan, started as a buyer. She asked a friend who was an eBay shopper to check to see if a particular item—something from a housewares line that happens to be a very popular eBay product—was up for sale. "She laughed and told me to go look for myself and hang onto my checkbook," Ayers recalls. She found what she was looking for and decided to try selling. "It was almost just for kicks—an 'I wonder if this rusty nail will sell' sort of thing. And I got hooked. I had a new baby at the time, so I sold some of her baby stuff. I sold one of her bouncy seats—it was used but in great shape—and I got more for it than a new one would cost at Target."

Before she began selling on eBay, Cindy Mayer had been a full-time nanny for 14 years and was looking for a change. She began selling on eBay when she wanted to buy a new set of dishes, and her husband told her to sell the ones she had first. "He gave me the push," she says. "I sold a service for 12, bit by bit, and that was my first experience on eBay. Then I was hooked." She formed Cindy's Collectibles and runs it as a steady part-time business. She loves shopping at flea markets and yard sales, and has a knack for spotting items that sell well on eBay.

Charlene Davis of Oviedo, Florida, began as an eBay shopper, then started selling some of her own things as well as items she found at garage sales. "Like so many people, I had plenty of things that I didn't want or need anymore, but they were in good condition, and I didn't want to just throw them out," says the owner of Busy Moms Recipes. "It sounds silly to say this, but I wanted my things to go to a good home. I didn't want them anymore, but I wanted someone who would appreciate them."

After a period of successfully selling collectibles on eBay on a part-time basis, Davis discovered Elance, which is the professional services part of eBay, and began selling her services as a virtual assistant and writer. She has also developed some of her own e-cookbooks to sell on eBay. "The opportunities on eBay are so tremendous and varied," she says. "It amazes me that I can sell my household odds and ends on the same site where I can also sell my professional services."

Gary and Susan Marler of Selma, North Carolina, consider their eBay business a hobby that allows them to earn extra cash. They began as shoppers and started selling to eliminate duplicates in their collections. "It's an easy business to do, and as you do it, you get better at it," Susan says. "For us, it has been a great way to make a little extra cash, and it has even helped us pay the bills as Gary was starting his upholstery business."

In Long Beach, California, Buz Moran takes a similar approach. He's a self-employed painter who sells collectibles on eBay as a profitable part-time hobby. "I was always a collector of stuff," he says. "EBay just happened, and I kind of fell into it like it was made for me." In his first six weeks of eBay selling, Moran made $1,800—pretty good wages for a part-time operation. "I was just buying things, not spending a lot of money but hitting home runs," he says. "I bought a bag of postcards for $5 and made more than $500 on them—one went for $142.50."

Tip of the Day

The FTC offers these quick tips for online auctions:

For Buyers

- ○ Identify the seller, and check the seller's feedback rating.
- ○ Do your homework. Be sure you understand what you're bidding on, its relative value, and all terms and conditions of the sale, including the seller's return policies and who pays for shipping.
- ○ Establish your top price, and stick to it.
- ○ Evaluate your payment options. If possible, use a credit card. It offers the most protection if there's a problem. Consider using an escrow service if the seller doesn't accept credit cards.

For Sellers

- ○ Provide an accurate description of the item you're selling, including all terms of the sale and who will pay shipping costs.
- ○ Respond quickly to any questions bidders may raise during the auction.
- ○ Contact the high bidder as soon as possible after the auction closes to confirm details of the sale.
- ○ Ship the merchandise as soon as you receive payment.

Cindy Hale is a full-time secretary with a thriving part-time eBay business called The Walker Avenue Attic. She had been buying on eBay for about a year when she decided it was time to clean out her attic, and it just made sense to sell those items on eBay. Besides, she says, "I had long wanted to do something that was just for me." The results of her eBay operation are a clean attic and a growing bank account.

What comes through loud and clear when these sellers talk about their busi-

Bright Idea

Make selling on eBay a family business. Get your spouse, kids, and other relatives involved in all aspects of eBay selling, from finding things to sell and handling the computer tasks necessary to post an auction to shipping the products and following up with top-notch customer service.

nesses is that eBay is about so much more than money. It's about the delight of finding a treasure and then matching it with the right buyer. It's about getting paid based on value and results, not the number of hours worked. It's about controlling your own destiny—and still more. EBay has made it possible for countless numbers of mothers to be at home with their children while earning a comfortable living—or supplementing the family's income. Sellers and buyers have connected to form business alliances as well as strong personal friendships. EBay users socialize, exchange gifts, and help each other out. After September 11, eBay members donated thousands of items to raise money for the families and communities hit hardest by the tragedy.

So if you're just looking for a place to do business, you've found it. And whether or not you were looking for more, you've found that, too.

What Do These Sellers Have in Common?

Your success on eBay will not be due to any one thing, but rather a combination of things. But here are a few things successful eBay sellers have in common:

- *They treat their eBay activities like a business.* You might get your start selling the occasional item on eBay the same way that you'd hold a garage sale once a year, not really caring how much you make as long as you don't lose money. But if you want a serious eBay operation that will earn you more than just pocket change, you have to treat it like a business. That means creating a separate business entity with a name, bank account, proper licenses, etc. It means finding suppliers you can count on and building solid relationships with them. It means shipping promptly, providing superior customer service, and leaving timely, accurate feedback.

- *They find a niche and build on their expertise.* It is impossible for any single person to be an expert in all the categories of merchandise on eBay. Successful eBay sellers specialize in one or two areas. "You can't possibly know the value of everything," says Mladjenovic. "The people who consistently make money, month in and

▲

month out, are the ones who specialize." They establish themselves as experts, and their knowledge is reflected in how their listings are written, the information on their About Me page, and how they respond to requests for additional information. They are generous in how they share what they know, whether it's information on their merchandise or assisting a new eBay buyer with making a purchase. Mladjenovic adds, "As soon as you start diverting from your specialty to something else, it's the same as if you started a brand-new business from scratch."

- *They are great communicators.* They know how to write auction listings that accurately and completely describe the product, shipping, payment options, return policy and other details. They respond to questions from bidders promptly, with complete and courteous answers. They communicate with winning bidders immediately at the close of the auction and maintain that communication until the transaction is complete.

- *They are persistent and learn by doing.* Successful eBay sellers don't give up easily. When an auction doesn't go as expected, they figure out what to do differently the next time for better results. They learn from their mistakes. And even when things are going well, they are always trying to figure out how to make them better.

From Recreation to Business

Selling on eBay is one of the easiest ways to turn your hobby or special interests into a business. Think about it: Whatever you enjoy doing, you have a degree of expertise and experience in—and you can translate that to dollars on eBay.

Most of the eBay sellers we interviewed had been buying and selling on eBay just for fun before getting serious about their businesses, and they all knew of others who had done the same thing. However, just because you enjoy your particular hobby and eBay shopping, don't make the mistake of thinking this will be just a lot of fun and games. One of the biggest pitfalls of taking this route to business ownership is failing to make the complete transition from amateur to professional.

No matter how enjoyable you find the process of buying and selling at auctions, you are selling a product your customers are paying money for, and you must respect the fact that this is a business transaction. You need to take yourself seriously and run your company like the professional operation you want it to be.

One of the most important issues you'll have to deal with is record-keeping. Whether you're new to online selling or you've been doing it for a while, consider these suggestions:

- *Open a separate checking account for the business.* Your bank account balance is a quick and easy way to see how well you're doing, but you won't have a clear picture unless you're using an account that is strictly for business income and expenses.

Linda Parker, a part-time Tustin, California, eBay seller, says the smartest thing she ever did in her business was opening that separate bank account. "For a long time, I just threw everything into our joint checking account, but it became very confusing with all these deposits and withdrawals, and I couldn't stand it anymore," she recalls. "Having everything separate makes it easy for me to tell whether I'm making as much money as I feel like I am. For instance, I may have a bunch of auctions end at the same time, and all the payments come in close together, and it seems like a lot of revenue. But with a separate account, it's easy to see what my costs were and how much real profit I made."

- *Get a credit card for the business.* You may not be able to get the card in the business name, and you may not be able to charge all your business purchases (for example, garage sale shopping requires cash), but at least have one card that is used exclusively for business expenses. This helps you keep your records in order and—if the card is in the business name—helps you establish business credit.

- *Invest in a retirement plan.* Beyond the long-term benefits, a retirement plan offers some short-term advantages. You'll not only reduce your current taxes, but if you are a homebased sole proprietor, the fact that you show a retirement plan on your income tax return indicates to the IRS that you are serious about your business, not just trying to take some questionable deductions.

- *Document your equipment.* Of course, anything you buy for your business after you start it is a deductible expense. However, if you purchased the equipment you use to sell on eBay (computer, printer, digital camera, scales, etc.) prior to starting your business and can prove the cost involved, you may be able to deduct those expenses on your tax return after you've formed your company. Talk to your tax advisor for specifics on how to do this.

- *Figure out how much it actually costs you to sell an item.* Besides the cost of the merchandise, calculate your overhead (the cost of maintaining a place to work); the time it takes you to write up your auction description, take photographs, and get the listing posted; packaging; freight; special handling; and any other expenses. Be especially careful about tracking your time; too many business owners in all industries fail to give their time the value it deserves.

Use the "Start-Up Checklist" on page 11 to make sure you tackle the goal of selling on eBay in an organized, well-thought-out way.

More Than Stuff and Services

In addition to being a great tool to use to start your own business, eBay is also a place where you might find an existing business to buy. Thousands of businesses are up for sale on eBay each month. Of course, many are iffy at best ("make money at home with your computer")—some listings in this category are instruction manuals and/or equipment rather than actual established businesses—but there are some real businesses for sale on eBay.

For a legitimate business or franchise, don't expect the process to be as quick as an auction for consumer merchandise. Buying or selling a business requires a lot of research, documentation, and negotiation. But eBay can still be a great way for people who are interested in buying or selling a business to hook up.

Buy First—Sell Later

Before you start selling on eBay, make a few purchases. "Before you try to sell anything on eBay, first take a look as a shopper for [what you want to sell] and see what other listings are like," says Mladjenovic. You'll learn firsthand how the system works and be able to put yourself in your customers' shoes. You don't have to spend a lot of money, and chances are you'll find things that you'd buy elsewhere anyway.

Another benefit of starting out as a shopper is that it gives you a chance to build a history under your user ID and earn some positive feedback (the value of which is explained in later chapters) so buyers will feel more comfortable with you later on when you start selling.

"Buy from a lot of experienced sellers and see how they handle things," advises Hale. "Copy the good ones and learn from the bad ones."

Start-Up Checklist

As exciting as eBay is, don't let it lure you into the deep end of the pool until you know how to swim. Use this checklist to get started.

❏ Decide what type of eBay business you want to start.

❏ Research your market.

❏ Set goals for your business.

❏ Develop a plan to achieve your goals.

❏ Learn how to use eBay.

❏ Do some shopping on eBay.

❏ Set up your payment system.

❏ Set up a record-keeping system.

❏ Obtain necessary licenses.

❏ Open a business bank account.

❏ Find sources for merchandise to sell.

❏ Set up your shipping system.

❏ Learn how to write a good auction listing.

❏ Get the necessary equipment (either scanner or digital camera) to take good pictures.

❏ Auction a few items to gain experience.

❏ Collect payment.

❏ Ship the merchandise promptly.

❏ Post feedback.

❏ Auction more items!

A Day in the Life
What It's Like to Be an eBay Seller

So what's it like to have a business that sells on eBay? The sellers we spoke with agreed: It's a lot of work—and a lot of fun.

Because there is no such thing as a typical eBay seller or a typical eBay business, there is no such thing as a typical day for an eBay seller. How they spend their days depends on the type of operation they have.

▲

Smart Tip

Tip...

As you establish yourself on eBay, work toward achieving PowerSeller status. When you do, you'll be eligible for special benefits, such as group health plans, prescription drug discounts, dental and vision coverage, and business insurance.

At IEP Visions, David Schultz is likely to spend his time on anything ranging from unloading trucks and readying shipments to traveling around the world looking for suppliers and negotiating with lenders for a line of credit. His days are always long and challenging—but, he says, also very rewarding.

Gotham City Online's Jonathan Garriss says both he and his partner typically work 12-hour days, six days a week. And though that sounds like a lot, he points out, "When we first started, we were working 15 or 16 hours a day, seven days a week."

With a staff of 20, Garriss doesn't spend his time listing auctions, taking pictures, or packing items to be shipped. Instead, he figures about 30 percent of a typical day is spent on operational issues, including monitoring financials, reviewing payments, and troubleshooting. The remainder of his time is focused on business development, building relationships with suppliers and customers, and developing systems to create a more efficient operation.

A snapshot of a smaller-scale operation looks both similar and different. Part-time eBay seller Linda Parker spends an average of two hours a day monitoring listings, answering questions from bidders, packing sold items, going to the post office, and doing other administrative chores. One or two days a week, she spends an additional three or four hours shopping at garage sales, estate sales, and thrift shops for things to sell. Her profits are modest—just a few hundred dollars a month—but she enjoys the work, the extra income, and the fact that she's able to be at home with her children every day.

Laurie Ayers averages three hours a day on eBay tasks. Cindy Hale spends about an hour a day online managing her auctions, corresponding with customers, and sending invoices. She spends about three hours each week on packing and shipping, and another five hours looking for merchandise to sell.

It's no surprise that the higher the volume of sales of the eBay sellers we talked to, the more systematic their approach is. Those who started out selling on eBay as a lark became more systematic as they got more serious about their businesses. Starting with a system will mean faster profits.

All About eBay

Mention eBay to ten people, and at least one of them is likely to say something like, "I went on the site once, and I was just overwhelmed. There was too much on it." The fact is eBay can be overwhelming at first, especially if you don't have any goals in mind when you first log on. But it doesn't take long to get comfortable with the site and all it has to offer.

Perhaps the most important thing to keep in mind about eBay is that it is constantly changing and evolving. In just the time it took to research and write this guide, we saw many changes and enhancements on eBay. And most of those changes involve making eBay more user-friendly and less intimidating.

Stat Fact

"The main strength of eBay is that there are millions of buyers and millions of sellers [on the site] 24 hours a day," says consultant Paul Mladjenovic. "But the main weakness of eBay is that there are millions of buyers and millions of sellers every day."

It's important to understand that eBay is not just one giant Web site—though it's definitely giant, it's actually a collection of sites offering sellers and buyers a variety of options. In addition to basic online auctions, those sites include:

- EBay Motors, where vehicles of all kinds are bought and sold.
- EBay stores, where sellers can set up a fixed site on which to sell their goods.
- PayPal, eBay's payment processing service.
- Sotheby's auctions, special online auctions.

Birds of a Feather

Many eBay sellers network with one another through various forums, groups, and e-mail lists. In addition to the opportunities on eBay itself, you can find online networking opportunities throughout the Internet. For example, single mom eBay seller Laurie Ayers is a member of two Yahoo! groups, "Staying at Home" and "Christian eBay Moms." She credits the support from those online communities as the primary reason for her eBay success and growth. "You've got to have support and encouragement," she says. "If you are left on your own, you are going to miss out on some valuable information." She says her online colleagues help motivate her when she's feeling down. "I've met some wonderful people online who I consider my friends, not just other sellers. There are more benefits to eBay than just moving your goods."

Sources for online groups include Google Groups (go to www.google.com and click on the groups tab), Yahoo! Groups (go to http://groups.yahoo.com), and Topica (go to www.topica.com).

- Charity auctions, to help people raise money for various causes.
- Live auctions, where buyers can bid on merchandise at a live auction as it's happening.
- Elance, eBay's marketplace for professional services.
- Wholesale, a special place on eBay for wholesalers.
- EBay Business, a marketplace especially for business buyers and sellers.

E Bay Policies

Complete details on current eBay policies can be found on eBay's Web site, so we won't go into all of them here. However, there are some you should know about before you begin buying and selling on eBay.

- *No kids allowed.* EBay requires that all users be at least 18 years of age. If your children want to sell things on eBay, you have to do it for them—and be responsible for the transaction.
- *Nonpaying bidder.* Bidders who win auctions but fail to follow through with the transaction face consequences. Nonpaying bidders will receive two warnings from eBay before they are suspended. Continued violations after reinstatement will result in an indefinite suspension. Of course, eBay understands that there may be legitimate reasons when a bidder doesn't complete a transaction, such as serious illness, emergencies, acts of nature, and computer problems. Nonpaying bidders can appeal the warnings they receive from eBay if they believe their circumstances warrant special consideration. When a bidder doesn't pay, the seller may request a credit from eBay for their final value fee.
- *Nonperforming seller.* Significantly misrepresenting an item by not meeting the terms and item description in the auction or failing to deliver an item for which you accepted payment is a violation of eBay policies and may also be considered criminal fraud.
- *Duplicate auctions.* A seller can have up to ten listings for identical items at any one time, but no more. EBay recommends selling identical items through Dutch auctions or eBay stores (covered later), rather than through individual auctions.
- *Outages.* When the eBay system experiences service outages, there is a structure in place to compensate users with credits on listing fees and/or listing extensions, based on the type and length of outage.
- *Soliciting off-site sales.* You may not circumvent eBay fees by using contact information obtained from eBay or any eBay service to complete a sale outside eBay.
- *Threats.* EBay policies prohibit making threats of physical harm to another user.
- *Profanity.* The use of language that is racist, hateful, sexual, or obscene in nature in a public area is prohibited on eBay.

- *Prohibited and restricted items.* As an eBay user, you are ultimately responsible for making sure that the items you buy and sell on eBay are both legal according to all applicable jurisdictions and permitted by eBay policies.

If you violate an eBay policy by either your action or the content of your auctions, you will typically receive an informational alert, explaining the violation and detailing any further action to be taken on your part. When deemed appropriate, eBay will end the auction and your listing fee will be refunded.

For serious or repeated violations of eBay rules, a user may be indefinitely suspended. Though indefinitely suspended users may be reinstated by eBay at its discretion, eBay also has the right to determine at any time that the suspension is permanent.

Suspended users may not register with eBay or use eBay's site in any way during the period of the suspension. When a user has failed to abide by this restriction, eBay will refer the situation for criminal prosecution.

It's a Very Safe Neighborhood

When you're considering opening a brick-and-mortar store, one of the things you think about when choosing your location is how safe the neighborhood might be. That's an issue you need to keep in mind when operating online, too. Though not totally without risk, as a venue for business operations, eBay is extraordinarily safe.

Most eBay users—like most people—are honest. But you don't have to just hope that you aren't dealing with the rare bad apple. EBay's feedback system gives you the opportunity to check the reputation of both buyers and sellers before you agree to a particular transaction.

In addition, all eBay transactions are covered by the eBay Fraud Protection Program, which reimburses buyers up to $200 (less $25 to cover processing) for items they don't receive or that they are dissatisfied with, if they are unable to work the problem out with the seller. EBay's SafeHarbor and Square Trade systems protect users when disputes arise or misuse of the system occurs.

Does eBay have its detractors? Certainly. Read some of the articles criticizing eBay, and you'll wonder how the company can stay afloat until tomorrow. But no company is perfect. When you look at the big picture, you'll see an organization that is financially sound with a clear plan for the future.

Is the eBay site absolutely perfect and flawless? No. As do all Internet sites, eBay suffers from occasional glitches and outages—that's why they have an outage policy.

However, it's up to you to monitor your auctions and report any problems. Also, if a service failure on eBay's part has a negative impact on your auctions, request the appropriate credit on your listing fees.

Now that we've completed this overview of eBay as an organization and an opportunity, let's get down to the nitty-gritty of doing business on the site. We'll begin with taking a look at what you can sell.

What Can You
Sell Online?

So what kind of merchandise should you sell? A lot of eBay sellers start out selling odds and ends they have around the house—and for good reason. For items that are in good condition, you'll probably get more money for them on eBay than at a garage sale. You probably have plenty of stuff that you'll never miss and you really don't need to store or dust anymore. And it's a relatively risk-free way to test the waters of eBay selling.

If you can't bear to part with anything you already have, start with products you know and have experience with. Choose things that have demonstrable market demand (that is, you know people are buying them). Don't make the mistake of selling only things you like, or the trendiest, coolest things you can find. If your goal is to make a profit—and it should be!—then you need to be selling things people will buy.

> **Fun Fact**
>
> What is surprising about eBay is not so much what people try to sell, but rather what people are willing to buy.

"Right now, the category with the greatest level of growth is eBay Motors," says eBay's Kevin Pursglove. (Note: We are not discussing the topic of selling cars online as an eBay selling opportunity because it's one thing to put your own personal car up for sale; it's altogether something else to start a business as a car dealer, and that's beyond the scope of this book.) "It's followed closely by computers, both desktops as well as laptops. Then consumer electronics; a broad category we refer to as 'books, movies and music'; sports; collectibles; and clothing and accessories." Each of those categories generates an estimated $1 billion a year in business, he says.

Just about anything you sell on eBay has the potential to be profitable—or not, depending on how you run your business. And eBay sellers have been amazingly creative at coming up with items to auction. Pursglove says one of his favorites was a woman who gathered up all the junk she found in the cushions of her sofa—gum wrappers, broken pencils, pen caps, peanut shells, etc.—and photographed it neatly arranged on a piece of velvet cloth, then put it up for auction. "I believe it ended up selling for something like $14 or $15," says Pursglove.

If you are considering selling an item, do a search on eBay and see if that product or similar ones are being offered for sale. If the market is saturated, you may want to reconsider trying to sell that product. At the same time, if absolutely no one else is offering the product for sale, you need to figure out if that's because no one else has thought of it, or if it's because no one will buy the item.

Depending on the category, seeing a lot of similar items up for sale may work in your favor or against you. For example, you may see a lot of the same item pop up in response to a search because people are buying. Or, observes antiques seller Sue Rudolph, "It might also mean the market is flooded and nobody wants it." You have to do more than just count the listings, she says. Look at the individual auctions and see if people are bidding on the items—that will give you an indication of the strength of the market. Then check the completed auctions for the item you searched for. That will tell you what the item is selling for (if, in fact, it's selling at all).

Collectible items that are not easy to find will naturally have less competition than commonplace merchandise and will probably bring in more money. However, if you're going to have a steady source of income, you also need a steady source of supply for whatever you're selling. Hard-to-find items may be more profitable on a per-sale basis, but focusing on those items may limit the number of sales—and therefore the amount of money—you can make on eBay.

If you really enjoy trading in those hard-to-find treasures, consider a mix of related items. Also, develop methods to reduce the amount of time you search for those items. For example, Laurie Ayers sells a lot of children's items—mostly things that are very common

Smart Tip

Brand names sell. New or used, people prefer to buy brands they recognize and trust. That means selling brand names is likely to be easier and more profitable than off-brands. Be sure to promote the brand in your auction's title.

but in relatively high demand. However, she has also found a niche with specific designer used men's Italian suits. While they aren't quite in the same category as a rare antique, they're still not extremely common. She finds them at thrift stores and occasionally at garage sales. "Once I found three Giorgio Armani suits for a total of $30, and I sold them for almost $600 total," she says. Because she knows exactly what she's looking for, her thrift store excursions are fast and efficient. Men's ties also sell well. "I paid a quarter for a tie once, and sold it for almost $40." She concedes that you often have to sort through a lot of junk to find such treasures, but if you've done your research and you know what you're looking for, you can usually do it quickly.

Deciding What to Sell

Whether you have a specific product line in mind or are still trying to come up with some ideas for what you can sell on eBay, consider these issues:

- *Cost.* How much will the item cost you? There's more to cost than simply the price on the item—do you have the cash required to make the purchase or are you going to have to borrow money (and therefore pay interest) to acquire the inventory? Will there be any additional expenses, such as shipping to you or repairs if the item is not in saleable condition?

- *Storage.* Do you have room to adequately and safely store the item while you are waiting for it to sell?

- *Shipping.* What are the labor and cost issues associated with shipping the item to your customer once it sells? Is it very fragile, an unusual shape, or extremely heavy? These are issues that can make shipping a challenge.

- *Product life cycle.* How long can you expect the demand for the item to continue? You may have something that is wildly successful today, but next year you won't be able to pay people to take it away from you. Beanie Babies and other fad collectibles are a great example of this. Some high-tech items are also at risk of having a short life cycle due to technology advances. If you pay attention to product life cycles, you can maximize your profits while the item is hot and avoid getting stuck with excess inventory when the demand declines.

Smart Tip Tip...

Consultant Paul Mladjenovic advises buying from people who do not understand the value of the items as well as you do (and are therefore willing to sell for less), but sell to people who do understand value and are willing to pay what the item is worth.

- *Season.* When you put an item up for sale on eBay, consider the time of year. Heavy coats and sweaters don't sell well in the spring and summer. Lawn and garden equipment is not going to move as well in the winter as it will in the summer. If you have room to store items, you can make a nice profit buying off-season items and holding them until they'll sell.

Where Will You Find What You'll Sell?

One of the most exciting things about selling on eBay is that merchandise that will sell for a profit is virtually everywhere!

- *Your home.* Start by looking around your own home at the stuff that's collecting dust on shelves or stashed in the back of closets, or in the attic or garage.

- *Flea markets.* Flea markets can be a tremendous source of bargain-priced merchandise that will sell on eBay.

- *Garage and yard sales.* Savvy eBay sellers can make a comfortable living spending one or two days a week shopping garage sales for items that will fetch many times what they cost when auctioned on eBay.

- *Estate sales.* If a professional is already handling the estate sale, you're not as likely to get really great bargains. But if you have access to a truck and storage, you can advertise that you buy entire estates. When you make such a purchase, select what will sell best on eBay, put those items up for auction, and then sell the rest through other channels.

- *Established retailers.* Stores need a way to move items that aren't selling. Once Gotham City Online was established, Jonathan Garriss was able to approach retailers and offer to help them solve their overstock problems by selling those items on a consignment basis on eBay. Eventually, he began purchasing that inventory outright.

Bright Idea

If you've received a gift you don't want and can't return, sell it on eBay.

Brother, Will You Take a Deposit?

If you find a great deal on something you know you can sell on eBay, but you don't have the cash to buy it outright, offer a small deposit to hold the goods for 10 to 14 days. Then post your auction for seven days, and when it closes and the item has sold, pick it up and pay the balance due then.

Do this only when you're buying from a seller you know and trust, and when you have carefully inspected the merchandise and are completely confident about authenticity and quality. If for any reason the item doesn't sell, you'll likely lose your deposit—but that's better than getting stuck with a high-priced item in your inventory that won't move.

- *Discount stores.* Look for clearance items at discount department and drug stores. Cindy Mayer of Cindy's Collectibles routinely buys infant's and children's items at the end of the season and stores them until the following year. "I buy out of season, and I have found great sales in drugstores," she says.
- *Friends and family.* Tell people you know not to throw anything away. Laurie Ayers says that members of her church will give her things they are going to throw away or donate to charity, and if she can sell them on eBay, she does.

Buying from Wholesalers

As your business grows, you may choose to start buying from wholesale sources and selling on eBay at retail. This can be very profitable, but only if you choose the wholesaler wisely.

The Internet is full of opportunities to buy lists of wholesalers, often for just a few dollars. Save your money. You can get the same quality of information (or maybe even slightly better) for free by using any of the popular search engines and plugging in keywords such as "wholesale," "manufacturer," or "drop ship." But even that is not the best route to take.

Instead, be more specific in your approach. Think about the type of products you want to sell, and then look for manufacturers, wholesalers, and distributors you can work with. Find companies whose products meet your quality expectations, that have prices and terms you can work with, and that deliver the service level you want to provide your customers. Get sample products so you can see the quality yourself. Some companies send free samples, while others charge a nominal fee—either way, don't try to sell something you've never seen. Be sure it is truly worth what you expect it to sell for.

David Schultz of IEP Visions buys most of his inventory of children's furniture from established manufacturers overseas. The items are made to careful specifications, inspected before they leave the plant, and then randomly tested after they arrive in the United States. Schultz refuses to accept any product that does not meet his high standards. "The last thing I would ever want on my conscience is someone's child getting hurt in something I built and sold to them," he says.

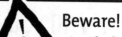

Beware!
Avoid wholesalers and distributors who charge an account setup fee or any other fee, or who want to restrict the products you sell. Legitimate companies make money from selling their products, not from charging administrative fees.

You may wonder why wholesalers aren't just selling their merchandise on eBay themselves for a greater profit. Some of them may be, but most legitimate wholesalers prefer to avoid the retail market and focus on the type of selling they do best, which is to sell their products to a retailer who will then sell to the public. Consultant Paul Mladjenovic explains that this is how they reach a wider market with fewer resources than if they tried to set up their own retail structure.

As you consider what to sell on eBay, keep this in mind: If you wouldn't buy shoddy, off-brand, imported merchandise for yourself, why would someone else want to buy it from you? "Don't go out there and find a liquidator store," advises Schultz. "There is a reason that product is being liquidated, and everybody on eBay has access to these products. You need to find your niche."

Be sure you're dealing with a true manufacturer, wholesaler, or distributor, and not another middleman who is marking up their prices and increasing your costs. Ask for and check references. You want to talk with others who are buying from these sources. In addition, check with the Better Business Bureau, any industry associations, the consumer protection agency of the state in which the supplier is located, and any other source that may be able to verify their claims.

Legitimate manufacturers, wholesalers, and distributors will also want information about you, including proof that you are a legitimate business and that you have any necessary licenses and tax identification numbers. You'll learn more about these issues in Chapter 8. A supplier who doesn't ask for this information is probably a middleman whose ethics couldn't stand up to moderate, much less close, scrutiny. Also, the discussion on purchasing in Chapter 11 applies not only to equipment for your business but to your inventory as well.

Keep this in mind: You're able to set up shop on the Internet for a very small investment, and your goal is to build a legitimate business. Don't you think scam artists know how easy it is to create an Internet presence? Of course they do. Don't become one of their victims.

Can You Compete Against the Superstores?

In many ways, the Internet is a great equalizer. When you're selling on eBay, you're keeping company with retail giants such as Sears, Sharper Image, Disney, Palm, Wickes Lumber, Motorola, the Golf Channel Pro Shop and more. And there's absolutely no reason you can't capture a reasonable share of the market these companies target.

Of course, you're also going to be competing against brick-and-mortar retail outlets, many with hundreds, if not thousands, of locations and the ability to buy in vast quantities at great prices. Don't let that scare you. At the same time, don't try to beat Wal-Mart at its own game. Don't try to sell the same products when there's no possible way you can match Wal-Mart's price and still make a profit. Instead, find a niche and a need that isn't being met by Wal-Mart (or other discount stores). Once you get a customer, offer service so great that they'll want to deal with you again and again.

Keep this in mind: Superstores carry a lot of products, but they can't possibly carry everything, and they usually only stock a few variations of each item. There are literally hundreds of thousands of items that are not being sold in a superstore that people want to buy.

Another point to remember: Don't make price your primary selling point. Certainly many people are looking for bargains when they shop on eBay, but not all eBay buyers are low-price shoppers. You should stress the benefits of your merchandise over and above price. There will always be someone who can sell for less than you.

Sharpen Your Negotiating Skills

When you're buying, you want to pay the lowest price possible—and when you're selling, of course, you want the highest price possible. That's why it's important that you know the market value of the products you intend to sell before you buy them. There's no real negotiation involved in selling through an eBay auction because you decide the minimum you'll accept, and the person who bids the highest amount above that wins. But when you're buying, your negotiation skills can mean the difference between a profit and a loss. In fact, more than one eBay seller told us their profits are actually made when they purchase their inventory—they just don't receive those dollars until the sale is complete.

Regardless of whom you're buying from—an individual, a small company, or a huge corporation—find out if there's any room for negotiation on the deal. The easiest way to do that is to simply ask. And if the merchandise price is firm, find out if you can deal on payment terms, shipping costs, delivery arrangements, or any other aspect of the transaction.

Always offer less than the asking price. You can always come up on your price if the seller refuses to budge and you still want the deal, but you can't go down once you've made an offer. Of course, don't just offer less—explain why you're offering less, and do it in a way that won't offend the seller. For example, don't say, "You want $200 for this? There's no way this junk is worth more than $150." Instead, say something like "I understand why you feel that this merchandise is worth $200, but considering the market and what it's going to take for me to resell it, I can only offer you $150." Then be quiet and wait for a response.

Smart Tip

When buying, know what your top price is before you begin negotiating, and don't go over it. When selling, know your minimum. Always keep these figures in mind during your negotiations.

Another effective technique is to let the seller name a lower price. Let's say the item you want is marked at $50. Just ask, "What's the lowest amount you'd take for this?" The seller may say, "$50," in which case you can counter with a lower figure, pay the asking amount, or walk away. Or the seller may say, "Well, I really want $50, but I'd let it go for $35." If you'd been hoping to get it for $40, you just made $5 on the deal.

In any situation, whether you're buying a salt shaker at a garage sale or a truckload of electronics from a major manufacturer, treat everyone involved with respect, listen to the other person's point of view and be sure you understand it correctly, and work toward a win-win solution.

Scavenger Hunt

As the economy cycles, it's easy to pick up bargains from distressed individuals and companies, and the Internet has made finding, buying, and selling these items much easier than in the past. You might think that easier accessibility and availability would drive prices down, but that's not necessarily the case. For example, let's say you live in a small Midwestern town and you find a piece of modestly priced art at an estate sale. You've done your homework and you recognize the value of the piece, but you also know that no one locally would be interested in buying it. However, with eBay and other online auctions, a collector in Los Angeles or New York who is willing to pay fair value can easily see the piece and buy it from you at a handsome profit. Remember that online auctions and other Internet sales avenues have opened up a wide range of markets that have a tremendous profit potential.

Consignment Selling

Consignment selling is a great way to make money on eBay without having to invest in inventory. You simply sell other people's stuff—typically antiques and collectibles, but it could be anything—and when the transaction is complete, you pay those people the amount for which the item sold, less a fee for your trouble. Consignment fees can range from as low as 10 percent to as high as 30 percent or more. When Garriss first started selling items his friends were cleaning out of their closets, he did it on a consignment basis with a 50–50 split of revenue after expenses.

Where can you find items to sell on consignment? Look around and be creative. Collectors who don't want to bother learning how to do online auctions may be happy to consign items to you for sale on eBay. Small specialty retail store owners or crafters might consider a consignment arrangement. Even thrift stores and retail consignment shops could let you sell some of their merchandise on eBay for them.

A good policy to use when selling on consignment is to insist on taking possession of the articles. Here's why: Let's say you find an antique desk the owner wants to sell. You sign a consignment contract, take pictures of the desk, and go home and list it on eBay, leaving the desk with the owner. When the auction is complete, the buyer sends you the money, and you call the owner to arrange to ship the desk. But he tells you he has changed his mind about selling.

Now you have a contract, which means you can take the issue to court and probably win. But is your buyer going to wait four to six months for you to get an injunction forcing the owner to turn over the desk? Probably not.

If you had possession of the desk before you put the auction up, this couldn't happen. Even if the owner changes his mind, you are in control when you have the merchandise in your own hands. Let's say that in the above scenario the owner called while the auction was in progress to say he wanted the desk back. You could explain that you have a contract and he is bound by it. Or, since the auction hasn't closed yet, you could offer to cancel the contract if the owner is willing to compensate you for your costs and time. However, once the auction has closed, you are contractually obligated to sell the item. So protect yourself by taking possession of consignment items.

"We take possession of all the merchandise we have for sale," says Garriss. "That's what allows us to do things like give special discounts

Beware!
When buying luxury items such as designer accessories and high-end jewelry to sell on eBay, ask to see the seller's driver's license and make a copy of it for your files. Also, have the seller sign a bill of sale that clearly describes the goods involved. This will protect you from criminal prosecution if it turns out that the merchandise has been stolen.

on shipping to people who buy more than one item. It also allows us to control delivery and customer service."

It's best to have a written agreement for all your consignment sales, even when you're dealing with a friend—or perhaps, especially when you're dealing with a friend. Writing it all down prevents any possible misunderstandings. Your agreement should include the commission amount (usually a percentage of the sale price), who pays selling expenses and what those are likely to include, a minimum sale price if applicable, when and how payment will be made, and anything else that may be relevant.

If you've agreed to sell a jumbled pile of items, consider charging an hourly fee for sorting and cleaning. If the owner balks, explain that you are a professional, this is your business, and if he doesn't want to compensate you fairly for your time, he can find someone else or do the job himself.

Special Rules for Selling Jewelry

The FTC requires that you make accurate and truthful claims about jewelry you offer for sale, and has issued guides to help you. The guides explain how to describe gold, silver, platinum, pewter, diamonds, gemstones, and pearls, and also outline what information you must disclose so that consumers are not misled. For example, if you are selling synthetic or imitation gemstones, you must clearly tell the consumer that the stone is not natural. If you are selling pearls, you must indicate if they are cultured or imitation. Copies of the FTC's Jewelry Guides can be obtained on the agency's Web site, www.ftc.gov.

Know and Heed the Restrictions

Considering the mind-boggling number and variety of items available on eBay, you might think that absolutely anything can be sold on this auction site. Not true.

EBay's policies very specifically bar the sale of any illegal item, and the company also has a detailed list of restrictions. (See "Is That Legal?" on pages 29–32 for a list of prohibited, questionable, and potentially infringing items.) Violate these restrictions, and at the very least your auction will be ended. At most, you'll find yourself suspended from eBay and possibly facing legal action. When the auction involves illegal activity, eBay will report the seller to the proper authorities.

For example, it didn't take long for items billed as debris from the space shuttle *Columbia* to appear on eBay—nor did it take long for those listings to be pulled from the site. Of course, taking part of an aircraft involved in an accident is a federal offense, which would also make attempting to sell pieces of *Columbia* subject to federal prosecution. But beyond the legal aspects, eBay often pulls listings that attempt to capitalize on a tragedy, such as when people attempted to sell pieces of the World Trade Center and Pentagon after September 11.

EBay's Pursglove says the company's customer service team regularly checks the site for merchandise that might be restricted or prohibited. They also respond quickly to user complaints about an item that may violate policies, so if you suspect a listing violates eBay's policies, report it.

Beware!
The Consumer Product Safety Commission bans the sale of goods that may be dangerous to consumers. Visit www.cpsc.gov for more information.

In the case of illegal items such as stolen goods, eBay cooperates with authorities. Pursglove says there have been instances where authorities have asked the auction site to leave a particular listing up in what amounts to a cyber-sting. Police officers bid on the item, making sure they win the auction. When they make arrangements to receive the merchandise, the arrest is made.

When it comes to dealing with policy violations, eBay tends to give users the benefit of the doubt. Typically, you'll get a notice explaining what you've done wrong and essentially telling you not to do it again. Repeated violations will likely result in a short-term suspension of your eBay account. Serious violations and chronic offenders may be indefinitely suspended.

Is That Legal?

The following list details items that are prohibited, questionable, and potentially infringing. If you're not sure your item is acceptable on eBay, check out the policies in the Help section of the site.

Prohibited

The following items may not, under any circumstances, be listed on eBay:

- Alcohol
- Animals and wildlife products
- Catalog and URL sales
- Counterfeit currency and stamps
- Counterfeit items
- Credit cards

▲

Is That Legal? (continued)

- ○ Drugs and drug paraphernalia
- ○ Embargoed goods and items made in prohibited countries
- ○ Firearms
- ○ Fireworks
- ○ Government IDs and licenses
- ○ Human parts and remains
- ○ Links to other Web sites (except as allowed in eBay's policies)
- ○ Lock-picking devices
- ○ Lottery tickets
- ○ Mailing lists and personal information
- ○ Plants and seeds
- ○ Postage meters
- ○ Prescription drugs and devices
- ○ Recalled items
- ○ Satellite and cable TV descramblers
- ○ Stocks and other securities
- ○ Stolen property
- ○ Surveillance equipment
- ○ Tobacco
- ○ Travel

Questionable

These items may be listed under certain conditions. Do further research before putting your auction up to be sure your item is allowed.

- ○ Artifacts
- ○ Autographed items
- ○ Batteries
- ○ Catalytic converters and test pipes
- ○ Compilation and information media
- ○ Contracts and travel-related tickets
- ○ Electronics equipment
- ○ Event tickets
- ○ Food
- ○ Freon and other refrigerants

Is That Legal? (continued)

- ○ Hazardous materials
- ○ Imported and emission noncompliant vehicles
- ○ International trading in any category that violates current laws
- ○ Materials targeted to mature (adult) audiences
- ○ Medical devices
- ○ Offensive material
- ○ Pesticides
- ○ Police-related items
- ○ Presale listings (items that are not in the control or possession of the seller at the time of the listing)
- ○ Slot machines
- ○ Used airbags
- ○ Used clothing
- ○ Warranties
- ○ Weapons and knives
- ○ Wine
- ○ Compilation CDs

Potentially Infringing

These items may be in violation of certain copyrights, trademarks, or other rights. EBay prohibits some of these items, regardless of the particular item's legality, because they almost always violate copyright and trademark laws. As with questionable items, do your homework before posting your auction.

- ○ Academic software
- ○ Beta software
- ○ Bootleg recordings
- ○ Downloadable media
- ○ Faces, names, and signatures
- ○ Games software
- ○ Items for which you disclaim knowledge of or responsibility for the authenticity or legality
- ○ Items or listings that misuse another product's brand name
- ○ Items that may violate a contract you have with another party
- ○ Mod chips

▲

Is That Legal? (continued)

- ○ Movie prints
- ○ OEM software
- ○ Promotional items
- ○ Recordable media
- ○ Replica and counterfeit items
- ○ Software or hardware that would enable a user to circumvent copy-protection features on video games, software programs, CD-ROMs, DVDs, or CDs
- ○ Tickets (travel)
- ○ Unauthorized copies

4

Technical
Basics

Not long ago, one of the biggest challenges of online auctions was the complexity of using them. Fortunately, times change. Today, eBay is an incredibly user-friendly system, whether you're buying or selling.

Longtime eBay seller Sue Rudolph recalls, "In the beginning, eBay was not user-friendly for sellers. It was easy to buy from, but hard to list on. And that intimidated me." Today, she says, you can easily learn to buy and sell on eBay, whether you're a computer novice or a computer nerd.

We're not going to spend time in this book walking you through the steps to register on eBay for two primary reasons. First, most people who are serious enough about learning to sell on eBay that they buy a book on the subject have already browsed the site and probably have already done a little buying and selling, so they already know how to register and use the site. Second, the eBay site itself will take you through the process quickly and efficiently. However, here's a piece of useful advice: If you happen to have a teenager in your home, as do many of the eBay sellers we talked with, just ask him or her to help you. Kids are a wealth of technological information.

If you haven't already registered on eBay, you should know that all registered eBay users are required to provide contact information—name, address, e-mail address and telephone number—when they register, and must maintain valid and current information on file. If your contact information changes, be sure to notify eBay immediately. You will also need to provide a credit card number and your checking account information. EBay uses this information to confirm your identity and therefore protect the integrity of their operation, and to collect auction fees.

EBay has strict rules about when user contact information is released. You can request contact information for eBay users who are involved in your current or recent transactions when that information is necessary to complete the transaction. For example, sellers can request contact information for all bidders in an active transaction and the winning bidder in a successful closed auction. Bidders can request contact information for a seller during an active transaction and if they are the winning bidder in a closed auction. Contact information may be useful if a bidder has a question about the item description and is unable to contact the seller by e-mail, if a seller needs information from a bidder to compute shipping charges or in some other way finalize the transaction, if a seller wants to verify the bidder by phone, or if a buyer or seller wants to resolve a listing-related dispute.

> **Tip...**
>
> **Smart Tip**
> Once your eBay account is set up, spend some time—at least several hours—browsing around, getting familiar with the site and its abundance of features before you begin buying and selling.

Your eBay User ID

Choose your eBay user ID thoughtfully. This is the name under which your reputation as a buyer and seller will be established. Though it's possible to change your user ID, it's not always a good idea. If you change your user ID, people who have done business with you before may not be able to find you by searching using your old user ID. One good thing about changing your user ID is this: Your history follows you, and your feedback remains intact, so any reputation you've worked hard to build will come with you no matter what your user ID is.

When choosing your user ID, consider the image it's likely to project to prospective customers. When Charlene Davis first starting buying and selling on eBay, she was doing it for fun and therefore chose a whimsical user ID that reflects her love of animals: theditzydog. However, that name just didn't work well for a serious professional bidding on projects on Elance, so she created a different user ID—cdavisadm—to use for that. "If I had realized what a tremendous opportunity eBay offered, I would have chosen a more professional-sounding user ID from the start," she says. Sellers are permitted to have more than one eBay account as long as their reasons are legitimate. However, there should never be any interaction between accounts belonging to the same person, especially in the areas of bidding and feedback.

Your user ID should also be easy to remember. A combination of letters and numbers that might make perfect sense to you (say, the first two letters of each of your children's names, followed by their birth months) could be hard-to-remember gibberish to

The Urge to Merge

EBay allows you to combine several user IDs, including feedback scores and comments, into one. If you do this, the old user IDs are no longer active and can't be used. EBay allows you to merge a maximum of two old user IDs into one, and the newly combined user ID cannot be merged again.

According to eBay's policies, to request a merge, you must meet the following requirements:

- ○ Be able to prove that you are the owner of the old and new user ID. Generally, that means the contact information on your old user ID needs to match that of the new user ID.
- ○ The old user ID must have no bidding or listing activity within the last 60 days.
- ○ You must have confirmed registration of the old and new user IDs.
- ○ The old user IDs must have a zero balance on the account; you cannot owe any seller fees on a user ID you merge.
- ○ You must use the same billing currencies (such as dollars or pounds) on both the old and new user IDs.

someone else. Cindy Mayer says she wished she had realized that when she used a combination of family initials to create her eBay user ID (jocin3) but later decided to call her business Cindy's Collectibles. "I would like to change my user ID, but when you do that, you get these little sunglasses (the shades icon) next to your name [for 30 days], and I really don't want people to lose track of who I am," she says.

Doing Research on eBay

Before you start buying or selling on eBay, you should be comfortable doing searches (or research) on the site—so practice before you have any money at stake.

You can do a basic search from just about any page on eBay. On eBay's home page, you'll see a box with a button next to it that says "Find it." On other pages, the button says "Search." When you type the search word or phrase for what you're looking for in that box, the system will check the titles of all currently open auctions and give you a list of matches.

For a more complete search, check the small box under the search box that says "search titles and descriptions." If you're searching from eBay's home page, click on "Smart Search" and then "search titles and descriptions." That will provide you with all the listings that include your search word or phrase in either the title or the body of the listing.

You should also get comfortable doing more advanced searches, such as by item number, seller or bidder user ID, category, location, price range, and payment method.

When you run across sellers who are doing the type of business that interests you, study what they do by searching according to their user ID. Look at their current listings, review their completed auctions, study their About Me page and their eBay store, and figure out how to apply their successful techniques to your own operation.

Along the same lines, monitor the activities of buyers who are shopping for the types of goods you want to sell. Who are they buying from? What are their bidding patterns? How much are they paying? What else are they buying that you might also want to sell? By clicking on their feedback number (the number in parentheses next to their user ID), you can see what other people have said about them as well as the items they've bought in the past. When the feedback list comes up, it will include the

Tip...

Smart Tip

While most items that are listed on eBay get sold, not all of them do. That means looking at completed auctions alone doesn't provide sufficient information to evaluate the selling potential of a particular item. You should be looking at bid history and final sale price of ended auctions. Just because something is listed doesn't mean there is a market for it.

item number of the auction; you can click on that number for details of what the merchandise was and what they paid for it. EBay keeps completed auctions clickable for a certain period of time, usually 90 days.

Studying completed auctions can tell you a lot about what is happening on eBay. Looking at minimum bids and Buy It Now prices can give you an idea of what sellers would like to get for their merchandise, but studying completed auctions tells you what buyers were willing to pay. Some sellers believe it's the best way to find out what is going on in the eBay marketplace.

Search Tips

Whether you're looking for something to buy or researching the market before putting an item up for sale, eBay offers these tips to help you find what you're looking for:

- *Try different search words.* Items can be described in a variety of ways. Imagine the words a seller might use to describe the item you're seeking, and try several different options and combinations. Use just two or three words at a time for the best results.

Abbreviation Station

As in any community, there's a "language" on eBay of common abbreviations used in auctions (especially in auction titles, where space is at a premium and character counts count!) and when buyers and sellers communicate. Here are some of the ones you'll need to know:

- ○ *COA:* Certificate of authenticity
- ○ *HTF:* Hard to find
- ○ *LN:* Like new
- ○ *MIB:* Mint in box
- ○ *MIMB:* Mint in mint box
- ○ *NIB:* New in box
- ○ *NOS:* New old stock (old stock that hasn't been sold or used)
- ○ *NR:* No reserve
- ○ *NWOT:* New without tags
- ○ *NWT:* New with tags
- ○ *OOP:* Out of print

- *Be specific, not general, and if appropriate, specify date, color, or brand.* To get targeted results from a search, be precise with your phrasing. For example, "crystal vase" will get better results than simply "vase"; "Waterford crystal vase" refines the search even more.
- *Add or remove the letter "s" for more results.* For example, a search for "necklaces" produces different results than a search for "necklace."
- *Understand how to use "and," "or," and "the."* When you put those words into a search, eBay's search engine looks for them just as it does any other word, so use those words only if you're searching for items containing those words, such as "Gladys Knight and the Pips" or "Truth or Dare." To search for one word or phrase that would be used in combination with another word or phrase, learn eBay's search commands, which can be found through the Help function.
- *Watch your punctuation.* Use punctuation in your search only if you expect it to be in the item title or description.
- *Consider browsing.* Browsing the category listing pages is like going on a treasure hunt; you never know what you'll find.

Common eBay Icons

As you browse around eBay, you'll see an assortment of icons that can be very informative. Here are some of the more common icons and what they mean:

- *Person with a sunburst behind their head.* This icon following a user ID indicates a new member. The icon alerts you that you might be dealing with a new eBay user who might need a little extra patience and assistance.
- *Two people with an arrow between them.* This is the "changed ID" icon and indicates a member who has changed his or her user ID within the last 30 days.
- *Picture frame.* A small picture frame means that the item is featured in eBay's gallery. It means you can see the item's photo in search results and browse listings.
- *Camera.* A camera means that a picture is included with the listing.
- *Burning match.* This signals a hot item. The burning match means an item has received more than 30 bids.
- *Auction paddle.* An auction paddle means an item is part of eBay Live Auctions.
- *Buy It Now.* The Buy It Now icon means the item has a set price for which it can be purchased immediately without going through the bidding process.
- *Wrapped present.* The neatly wrapped present means the seller wants to highlight the item as a potential gift.
- *About Me.* A "me" after a user ID indicates that user has an About Me page with more information about his or her eBay operation. The About Me icon is also a link to the user's About Me page.

- *PowerSeller.* A blue silhouette in a gold star next to the words PowerSeller indicates that this user has achieved a certain sales volume and performance status within eBay.
- *Rising sun.* A rising sun icon next to a listing indicates that the item has been listed within the past 24 hours. New-item icons are automatically removed after the listing is 24 hours old.
- *New!* The yellow "new" icon indicates a new service or feature on eBay.

How to Sell on eBay

Selling on eBay is really very simple as long as you approach it systematically. The first step is, of course, to set up a seller's account. Then decide what payment forms you'll accept (see Chapter 9) and set up those accounts. Do this *before* you start listing items for sale.

Next, choose a selling format. The most popular is, of course, eBay's standard online auction format (Chapter 5 discusses this in greater detail), but you can also sell through your own eBay store (see Chapter 6) or set a fixed price for your item. Then select your category, write a great title and description, decide how long you want your listing to run, when it should start and end, what your minimum bid will be and other pricing details, add pictures, enter your payment and shipping information, and then very carefully review your listing. If everything is accurate, submit your listing.

There are more ways than just this one to start an auction on eBay, and sellers who do more than a little bit of part-time selling on eBay usually use a bulk-listing tool to start their auctions. This makes it possible to start multiple auctions at one time and streamlines the listing process. EBay provides two primary listing tools, Turbo Lister and Seller's Assistant, and these are discussed in depth in Chapter 7.

Most sellers monitor their auctions to see how many people are looking and how the bids are going. Prospective bidders may have questions about your item. EBay allows them to contact you via e-mail from the listing, and you should answer those questions as quickly and completely as possible.

Once your auction has ended, communicate with the winning bidder regarding payment, shipping instructions, and any other details that need to be handled. When you've received payment, ship promptly and leave feedback for the buyer. For more on feedback, read Chapter 7.

Stat Fact

In a traditional live auction, the auctioneer will keep accepting higher bids until the bidders stop bidding. An online auction ends at a particular time, so the bidding may be fast and furious in the closing minutes.

Learn the Language—HTML, That Is

Hypertext Markup Language, or HTML, is a simple programming language that is commonly used to create Web pages. You can use HTML to jazz up your eBay listings.

By putting codes within the "less than" and "greater than" symbols (< and >), you can tell text how to appear in your listing. For example, inserting <b> before text will make that text bold—until you enter the command to end the bolding, which is </b>.

When HTML codes (also known as tags) are inserted in text, it can look confusing until you put the text up on eBay or on a Web site, and the coding disappears but the text shows up with all the attributes you want. As you're creating your document, you may find it easier to work with if you add blank lines so you can see the coding more clearly. Those extra lines will be ignored when the HTML is interpreted.

EBay's site includes basic information about how to use HTML in your auction listings. You can also enter "HTML" in any search engine, and you'll find a wide range of online resources that will explain how to create HTML documents.

It's entirely up to you whether or not you use HTML in your auctions, and it's certainly not mandatory. Many eBay sellers use only simple text and photos in their auction listings, and they run profitable businesses. It's possible to go overboard with HTML, of course. Too many colors, too many fonts, too many different font sizes, etc., can get a little busy. Sometimes, the simpler an auction looks, the better.

Your Own Web Site

Bright Idea

Use your Web site to take advantage of affiliate programs. This is when you put a link to someone else's site on your Web site. If a visitor to your site clicks on that link and then joins the affiliate's program, you earn a commission. Be careful to choose affiliate programs that will be of interest to your target audience.

A Web site lets you sell products to a potentially different market than you'll reach on eBay. You can put a link on your site to your About Me page on eBay (or put a link to your Web site in all your auction listings), and some people may decide to skip the auction process and buy directly from you. You'll also attract Internet shoppers who don't use eBay.

Unless you are extremely proficient with Web design, hire a professional to put together an attractive, user-friendly site for you. For more on setting up a Web site, read Chapter 9 in *Start-Up Basics*.

Auction Management Software

While it's possible to have a profitable business selling on eBay without using any additional software, good auction management software will save you time and money, make you more efficient, and improve the level of customer service you offer. "It's very easy to learn eBay," says Gotham City Online's Jonathan Garriss. "It's very easy to sell an item on eBay. It's very difficult to do that efficiently." Supplemental software helps automate your processes to improve productivity and profitability. Auction management software is also helpful if you use other online auction sites in addition to eBay.

"There are a lot of people who get to a certain point where they simply cannot manage the listing of the merchandise on a manual basis," says eBay's Pursglove. "They need automated tools and software that can help them do everything from listing the items to handling the billing and paying the fees."

Of the eBay sellers we spoke with, the smaller ones tend to do things manually or use eBay's tools, while the larger ones use auction management software or have developed their own systems to manage their operation. "We are all about automation," Adam Ginsberg says—which is understandable, considering ZBilliards' sales volume.

> **Tip...**
>
> **Smart Tip**
>
> Once you've mastered the basics of operating on eBay, begin exploring options and tools to make you more efficient and profitable, and increase your volume.

You can purchase software or subscribe to an online service that will help you create your listings, launch them manually or automatically at the time you determine, manage your photographs, count how often your listing is viewed, send e-mails to buyers, manage inventory, print shipping labels, post feedback, and more. Some auction management service providers also offer payment processing. Auction management software will also provide you with reports that will help you manage your business more efficiently.

5

EBay Auctions
The Foundation of eBay Selling

To put something "up for auction" on eBay is not complicated or difficult—however, it's not quite as simple as those three words might sound. The online auction world is not a one-size-fits-all proposition. Under the broad category of auctions falls a variety of types, and you need to choose the one or ones that will get the best results for you and your particular products. As you're getting started, you may want to do some experimenting with the different types of eBay auctions to see how they work.

Let's begin by taking a look at the different types of eBay auctions.

Reserve Price Auction

Auctions that have a hidden minimum price are known as reserve price auctions. The reserve price is the lowest amount the seller is willing to accept for the item. Buyers are not shown what the reserve price is; they only see that there is a reserve price, and whether or not it has been met. If the reserve price is not met, the seller is not obligated to sell the item. To win the auction, a bidder must meet or exceed the reserve price *and* have the highest bid.

In a reserve price auction, bids are made as usual, but bidders receive a notice if their bid does not meet the reserve price. Once the reserve is met, the item will sell to the highest bidder when the auction closes.

Sellers see reserve pricing as a way to protect their investment without revealing upfront how much they want to get for the item. Charlene Davis has used reserve prices and says they've always been met. But David Schultz, whose IEP Visions sells children's furniture, says many bidders avoid reserve auctions because they can't tell what the lowest winning bid needs to be, and they figure bidding on a reserve auction is a waste of time.

Buy It Now

This is a feature you can add to a traditional auction format that gives bidders the option to bid on your product or to buy it immediately. With Buy It Now, you set the price you're willing to sell for, and bidders can either place a bid for less than that amount (but at or above your starting price) or win the auction instantly by paying the Buy It Now amount. When a bidder agrees to the Buy It Now price, the auction ends. If someone places a bid below the Buy It Now price, the Buy It Now option disappears.

Here's how it works: Let's say you post an item with a Buy It Now price of $15 and an opening bid of $3. If someone is willing to pay $15 and there are no other bids, the auction is over as soon as that person agrees to buy the item for $15. Or, someone can bid $3, the Buy It Now option goes away, and the auction proceeds like any other auction. That $3 might be the only bid you'll get, or bidding could drive the final sale price above $15.

Cindy Hale of The Walker Avenue Attic likes the Buy It Now feature and says it works well if you don't get greedy when you set your BIN price. She often sets her BIN price just slightly higher than the opening bid amount. "I get a lot of quick sales that way," she says.

Tip...

Smart Tip
EBay assigns an item number to each listing, and you can look up items by that number.

Schultz takes a different approach, setting his BIN prices at what is close to full retail. For example, he might set the minimum bid for a crib at $99, with a Buy It Now price of $229. If he gets anything in-between, he's made a profit and the customer has gotten a good deal and knows it.

Fixed-Price Listings

EBay's fixed price format allows users to buy and sell items immediately at a set price, with no bidding or waiting. You can sell more than one item in a fixed price listing, which saves you time and money.

Private Auctions

In most auction formats, anyone looking at the item can see the user IDs of the people who are bidding on it. With the private auction format, however, the bidders' user IDs are not seen on the item or bidding history screens. When the auction is over, only the seller and winning bidder are notified via e-mail.

This format is useful when you believe your prospective bidders may not want their identities disclosed to the general public. Well-known collectors often prefer private auctions. A common use of this format is for collectibles when just the knowledge that a certain collector is bidding on an item would greatly increase the interest in the auction. Private auctions are also appropriate for items not intended for mass viewing, such as adult material.

Dutch Auctions

When a seller offers two or more identical items for sale in the same auction, it's known as a Dutch (or multiple item) auction. There can be many winners in this type of auction. For sellers, the power of a Dutch auction is that it allows you to sell large quantities of a single item with just one listing.

When you post a Dutch auction, you decide on your minimum bid amount (the lowest price you're willing to accept) and list that along with the total number of identical items you have available. Bidders specify the number of items they're interested in and the highest price they're willing to pay per item.

What makes Dutch auctions interesting—and complicated—is that all winning bidders pay the same price per item, which is the lowest successful bid. Most commonly, all buyers pay the starting price. But if there are more bids than

> **⚠ Beware!**
> You can't bid on your own auction, but if you change your mind about selling your item before the auction ends, you can cancel all bids and end the auction early. Once the auction ends with a bidder, you are contractually obligated to complete the sale.

items, the items will go to the earliest successful bids at the close of the auction. Bidders may bid on any quantity but have the right to refuse partial quantities.

Here's how it works: You have 50 toy airplanes you're willing to sell for $5 each, but if you could get more, you'd be pleased. So instead of listing 50 separate auctions (which would also mean 50 separate listing fees, and you'd have to space those auctions out over a period of time because of eBay's restrictions on the number of simultaneous auctions for identical items) or a fixed-price auction (which would eliminate the possibility of the items selling for more than your starting price), you put the toy airplanes up as a Dutch auction with a starting price of $5 each.

If 50 people bid $5 on one airplane each, then at the close of the auction, those 50 people would be the winning high bidders, and each would receive one toy airplane for the price of $5.

But Dutch auctions aren't always that simple. If any one of those people had bid more than $5, everyone would still only have to pay $5. For the final price to be more than $5, all the winning bidders would have had to bid more than the starting amount. So if 100 people placed individual bids on those toy airplanes, and 20 of those bids were for $8, 30 were for $7, 15 were for $6, and the remaining 35 were for $5, the toy airplanes would be sold to the first 50 bidders for $7 each, because that was the lowest successful bid. The lowest successful bid was $7 and not $5 because there are only 50 airplanes and 100 bidders. You start counting back from the highest bid until you reach the number of bids that matches the number of items; then everyone pays that bid price.

Here's another possible scenario: Let's say Sam bid on 25 of the toy airplanes at $5 each, then Mary bid on 10 of the airplanes at $5 each, George bid on 10 of them at $6 each, Cathy bid on 10 at $5 each, and Harry bid on five at $5. Even though George bid $6, all the toy airplanes will be sold for $5 each, because that was the lowest successful bid. So Sam will get his 25, Mary will get her 10, George will get his 10, but there are only five left for Cathy. Cathy has the option to accept the five, but she can also refuse them because she wanted 10. If Cathy refuses the five, the seller can then go to Harry to complete the sale.

Bidders in Dutch auctions do not receive outbid notices from eBay, nor can they use eBay's proxy bidding system (which allows a bidder to enter a hidden maximum bid), so they must actively monitor the auction and rebid if necessary.

The most important things to keep in mind when using the Dutch auction format are that the items in a single Dutch auction must be absolutely identical, and the auction itself must be listed in the appropriate category.

Don't be tempted to try something known as "Dutch avoidance"—that is, listing a single item and offering additional identical items for sale in the item description. Sellers who do this typically instruct buyers to indicate the number of items they want and offer those at the same price as the item in the listing. Sellers who successfully do this manage to avoid paying the full final value fee (see below) for everything they sell, but the practice is dishonest and against eBay policy. Listings that violate this guideline will be ended by eBay.

> **Stat Fact**
> EBay users create 1.7 million new listings each day.

Live Auctions

This particular type of auction is of more interest to an online buyer than to a seller, but it's something you should know about. EBay's live auctions feature allows you to bid real time on auctions that are happening on the floor of offline auction events. You can place absentee bids, bid against the floor or just watch the auction—all from the convenience of your home or office. For more information, go to www.ebaylive.auctions.com.

Restricted-Access Auctions

This category makes it easy for buyers and sellers to find or avoid adult-only merchandise. To sell, view, and bid on adult-only items, users must have a credit card on file with eBay. Items listed in the adult-only category are not included on eBay's New Items page or the Hot Items section, nor are they available by any title search. Failure to list an adult-only item in the correct area could result in a suspension.

EBay's policies stipulate that all users must abide by all applicable regulations regarding the sale and distribution of adult materials, and any violation of the law is also a violation of eBay's user agreement, and will be treated accordingly.

Auction Fees

While eBay is free to buyers, sellers must pay to use the site. The pricing structure is very similar to traditional auctions, although the amounts are very modest. The different types of fees are explained here, but eBay periodically adjusts its fee structure, so you should check the site for the current fee amounts.

Insertion Fees

You must pay a nonrefundable insertion fee or listing fee for listing your item on eBay. This fee will vary with the type of listing.

- *Single quantity, online auction listings.* The insertion fee is based on the minimum bid you set for your item—the lower your minimum bid, the lower the fee.
- *Reserve price auction listings.* The insertion fee is based on the reserve price of your item—as with the minimum bid, the lower your reserve price, the lower the fee. You will also be charged a reserve price auction fee, which is refunded if your item sells.
- *Dutch auctions and multiple item fixed-price listings.* The insertion fee is based on the opening value (the minimum bid or the fixed-item price multiplied by the quantity of items) of your merchandise.

Final-Value Fees

When your item sells, eBay will charge a final-value fee based on the final sale price. For regular and reserve price auctions where the reserve price is met, the final-value fee is determined by the winning bid. For Dutch auctions, the final-value fee is determined by multiplying the lowest successful bid by the number of items sold. For multiple item fixed-price listings, the final-value fee is calculated by multiplying the Buy It Now price by the quantity of items sold.

For general merchandise listings, the final-value fee is a percentage that drops as the closing value increases. For vehicles and real estate, the final value fee is a flat amount.

A final-value fee is not charged if there were no bids on your item, or if you listed a reserve price auction and the reserve price was not met, and therefore the item did not sell. But if you have bids on the item, and those bids meet your reserve price if you had one, you will be charged a final-value fee whether or not the buyer pays for the item and completes the transaction.

If something goes wrong after the auction ends and the sale doesn't go through, you can request a refund of your final-value fee. The circumstances under which eBay will consider issuing a credit for the final-value fee include if the buyer didn't pay or if the buyer paid but returned the merchandise and you issued a refund.

Bright Idea

Watch for eBay listing specials. Periodically eBay will offer steep discounts on various listing features to encourage you to try them. (Sometimes eBay charges only a penny to use the Gallery feature, when it normally costs 25 cents.) Take advantage of these money-saving offers.

Listing Upgrade Fees

EBay offers sellers a variety of ways to promote their merchandise through listing upgrades. The fees vary from a nominal amount (as low as 5 cents) to substantial (approximately $100 or more, if you combine features), and are nonrefundable.

Listing upgrade features include:

- Home Page Featured
- Featured Plus!
- Highlight
- Bold
- Gallery
- Gallery Featured
- List in Two Categories
- 10-Day Duration
- Scheduled Listings
- Buy It Now
- Gift Services

> **Bright Idea**
>
> Before you list, find out what else is on the market and how it will affect your listing. When Sue Rudolph sells an antique or a collectible, she doesn't want a dozen other items like it up for auction at the same time. For example, she checked eBay before she listed a Royal Doulton Princess Diana doll, and the same doll was already listed. She listed her doll after the other auction closed.

See "Marketing Your Auctions" on page 54 for more information on how to use these listing upgrade features to enhance your auctions and increase your income.

PayPal Fees

PayPal is an eBay service that provides a fast, easy, secure way for people to exchange funds online. There is no charge to open a PayPal account or to make payments using PayPal. Payments can be made by withdrawing money from deposits made to your PayPal account, by withdrawing money from your own bank account through PayPal, or by using a credit card through PayPal. Personal accounts are free but cannot accept credit card payments. PayPal's Premier and Business accounts can accept credit card payments but charge a fee to receive funds. Fees are assessed at the time of the transaction.

Timing Is Everything

Experienced bidders often wait until the final hours or minutes of an auction to bid to avoid driving the price up too early. Those final hours are also the time when auction fever can strike, with bidders in fast and furious competition over who is going to purchase your items. This is why you need to keep timing in mind when you put your auctions up.

The most popular online shopping days are Saturday, Sunday, and Monday, and the least popular are Thursday and Friday. Time your auctions to end on one of those popular shopping days to maximize bidding activity. EBay offers auctions with three-, five-, seven- and ten-day durations. Part-time eBay seller Buz Moran prefers five-day auctions. "You get a quicker return. Start it on Tuesday and it ends on Sunday," he says.

If you're using ten-day auctions, list them so they cover two weekends, which gives you the benefit of high weekend traffic twice.

Capture late bids by scheduling your listings to close at hours that are convenient for your target market. Close auctions for consumer items and collectibles during evening hours, when more individuals are likely to be online shopping and bidding. For items that are more appealing to a business or dealer, close your auction during normal work hours.

The eBay Scheduler lets you choose the day and time your auctions begin, so you can prepare your listings at your convenience and still have an optimum close date and time. There is an extra charge for using this service. Other auction software programs will do the same thing.

Feature Presentation?

When writing up your auction listings and product descriptions for items in your eBay store, pay attention to the difference between features and benefits. "Benefits are what people will derive from a product, and features are just telling you the nuts-and-bolts description of the product," says consultant Paul Mladjenovic. Don't just list a product's features; be sure to include the benefits as well.

For example, the features of a multivitamin are its ingredients; the benefits are that you will feel better, live longer, be healthier, or whatever. The features of a set of dishes include the color, the material, and the pattern; the benefits may be that your dinner table will look elegant or that, because the dishes are very durable and will stand up to rough treatment, you'll save money by not having to replace them soon.

You must list features because those are the facts about your items. Just be sure that for every feature, you list at least one corresponding benefit.

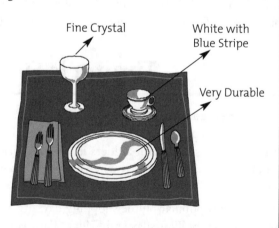
Fine Crystal

White with Blue Stripe

Very Durable

Getting Your Auction Listed on eBay

There's a very logical sequence to getting an auction posted on eBay. Learn how to do it manually before you graduate to automated systems. Start by choosing your listing type from the options we've discussed. If you're unsure, consider what types other successful sellers have used for similar products.

Determine Your Starting Price

This is the lowest price you're willing to accept for your item (unless you have specified a reserve price), and this is the amount at which bidding starts. Be reasonable when calculating this figure. Certainly you want to make a profit on what you sell, but sellers have found that setting the starting price too high often discourages bidding. A lower starting amount may attract a flurry of initial bidders who will quickly drive the price up. If you are using a fixed-price format, you'll enter a Buy It Now price. See the pricing section in Chapter 9 for tips on how to determine your starting price.

Write Your Title

EBay allows 45 characters (letters and spaces) for your listing's title, and you need to make each one count. Your title must make a prospective bidder want to learn more about your auction.

It helps if your headline is clever and catchy, but above all, it must be accurate and factual. Tricking people into looking at your auction because they think it's something else won't get you more bids—but it *will* make people mad, and they'll remember that the next time they look at one of your auctions. Also, misleading titles are against eBay policy and could result in eBay ending your auction early. Though you might see them often, devices such as "L@@K" and excessive exclamation points don't attract additional bidders, but they do brand you as an amateur. Use all caps sparingly and only to make certain words stand out.

Your title needs to include the key words that someone who is looking for your item might conduct a search for. If you have room, include a related word so your listing will come up in more searches. For example, let's say you're selling a pair of candleholders. Your title could read "Stunning Antique Cut-Glass Candleholders." Not bad, but if you wrote "Cut-Glass Candleholders for Tapers, Candles," you would come up in searches for cut glass, candleholders,

Smart Tip

If the item you are selling is related to a particular event, such as tickets for a performance or a holiday, be sure your auction closes in time to allow shipment to the buyer.

tapers, and candles in general. Certainly if someone is searching for the size or style of candles that your candleholders accommodate, they might be interested in another pair of candleholders, even if they weren't initially searching for them. So be creative in the language you use in your titles. Think of everything your item relates to, and figure out how you might be able to get as many of those words as possible into your title.

Bright Idea

Some (if not most) buyers only look at listings with photos, so having a photo in your listing will likely increase the number of people who view your auction.

Your title should also indicate why your listing is special. Consultant Paul Mladjenovic uses a picture of Frank Sinatra as an example. Let's say you have a photograph you believe will appeal to people who collect Sinatra memorabilia. The headline "Frank Sinatra Photograph" will probably get some hits. But "Rare Photo: Frank Sinatra at Last Concert" will probably attract more interest from serious collectors. However, use the word "rare" sparingly and only when truly accurate. It's a commonly overused term in eBay auctions.

If you are selling a brand-name item, include the brand name in the title. However, do not compare brand names in your title; only include the brand of the item you are offering. If the item is clothing or something that comes in different sizes, indicate the size.

Write Your Description

Investing time in writing a good description will pay off in the price you receive. A well-crafted description gives bidders the information they need to make a buying decision, as well as demonstrates that you are a professional, conscientious seller. A sloppy, incomplete description will not inspire confidence in prospective bidders. You need to tell what you are selling clearly, completely, and using powerful, persuasive words. Look at your items as though you have never seen them before and know nothing about them. Then write a description that will make someone want to own what you're selling.

Your description should include:

- the name of the item;
- what the item is made of;
- when and where it was made;
- who made it (company, artist, designer, author, etc.);
- what condition it's in;
- weight, size, and/or dimensions;
- notable features or markings; and
- any special background or history.

Everything in your description should be true and accurate. You might also add a personal touch to your description; many sellers have found that doing so can increase bids and sales. For example, specifically say what you like about the item, who it would appeal to and why, and how it could be used. If you know an interesting story about the item, share it. For example, you may have an antique silver spoon that was once owned by Henry VIII. You'll probably get a decent price if you just describe it as an "antique silver spoon," but add the detail about its previous owner, and the value increases.

If the item is not in perfect condition, be honest. Describe any scratches, chips, stains, and other imperfections. Failing to do this can create a disgruntled customer and result in negative feedback and perhaps returned merchandise.

Although bidders can e-mail you using a link on your listing page if they have any questions, don't assume you'll hear from them if they want more information. Though some will write, many will just bid on something else that's described better.

Think about how you would react to short and obviously incomplete descriptions. A bid is a contract—are you willing to make a commitment to buy something you don't know much about? Do you wonder if the seller is trying to hide something?

Something else to keep in mind as you write your description is not to do something known as "keyword spamming," which is against eBay's listing policies. This means you shouldn't include words in your description that are not actually related to your item just because you think buyers would find those words appealing and because they are words a search would pick up. For example, don't write, "This dress is an Anne Klein style," unless it really is an Anne Klein design.

At the same time, use as many legitimate search words and phrases in your description as possible so your item will come up when bidders are searching.

You can also use your description to add details about shipping costs, payment terms, and any other details you think may be of interest to a bidder. Even if you plan to charge actual shipping, it's always a good idea to include at least an estimate of the shipping costs so bidders aren't surprised when the auction is over. For example, since the post office charges by weight and distance, you can calculate the postage to a nearby ZIP code, and then to one far away, and write in your description: "Buyer pays actual postage. Estimated cost will be $5 to $8 via USPS parcel post (5 days) or $7 to $12 via Priority Mail (2 to 3 days)." Also, let bidders know if there are any restrictions on where you will ship, such as U.S. only, U.S. and Canada only, or to certain international locations.

When you're finished, proofread and spell-check—and then proofread again.

Choose the Right Category

With millions of items up for sale at any given moment on eBay, putting your auction in the correct category is essential. While many bidders will do searches looking for specific items, others just browse categories looking for any item that interests them. One of the biggest mistakes unsuccessful eBay sellers make is listing in the wrong category.

Browse around eBay and find items that are similar to what you want to sell, and see what categories they're listed in. Check completed auctions to see what the final sale price was, and look for trends that would indicate that listing an item in one particular category gets better results than another.

Marketing Your Auctions

EBay offers a wide range of services you can use to market your auctions. Some are free; most are available for a nominal fee.

A featured auction is given extra exposure in the "Featured" sections at the top of the listings pages. Schultz says this is one of his favorite marketing tools. At any given time, he might have 300 or more items up for sale on eBay, and he'll run 20 percent as featured auctions. The cost to run a featured auction often eats up a significant amount of Schultz's profit on that particular item, but the exposure attracts buyers to his other nonfeatured auctions and generates substantial revenues that way. It's an approach very similar to the loss leaders you see in grocery stores—when popular items are sold at cost or below just to get people into the store.

The Gallery feature places a photo along with your title in search results. This allows viewers to see your item without having to click on the full listing. An attractive gallery photo will make your listing stand out. Garriss says gallery images have worked well for Gotham City Online. Single mom Laurie Ayers says they are well worth the extra charge because they "grab attention." And eBay says listings with gallery photos get a lot more bids than those without gallery photos.

If you think your item would make a good gift, use eBay's Gift Services feature. The gift icon (a wrapped package) will appear next to your listing on search and browse pages and tells buyers if you offer gift services such as gift wrap, gift cards, express shipping, and shipping directly to the gift recipient. Your item description should include details of and charges for the gift services you provide.

You can also dress up your listing with highlighted and bold text in the headline, and you may want to list your item in two different categories for additional exposure.

In addition to promoting your auctions within the eBay community, consider using your own

Beware!
While it's good to model your own eBay operation after those of successful sellers, don't use another user's images or descriptions in your listings or About Me page without that user's permission.

personal or professional network as well. If you belong to a club or have friends who share a common interest and you are selling something that may appeal to that group, let them know about it. Set up an automatic signature on your e-mail that includes a notice about your auctions at the end of every message you send.

> **Fun Fact**
>
> When a nonreserve item receives more than 30 bids, eBay marks that item with a lighted match icon that shows it as a "hot item" in search results.

When you post your auctions, make your listings sparkle by adding bold, italics, and color to your text. Use HTML, which was discussed in Chapter 4. But be cautious when adding features that include motion and sound. For users with dial-up connections, these listings can take a long time to load, and some bidders may opt to move on to another listing rather than wait. Also, while sound may be cute and possibly even entertaining, it could end up being a tattletale feature if someone is browsing around eBay when they should be doing something else (like working). Moran says, "My philosophy is to keep it simple and quick."

The Bidding Process

For most auctions, the bidding process is fairly straightforward. You set your minimum bid, and people interested in buying your merchandise place successively higher bids until the auction closes. Beyond that, however, are some details about bidding you need to know.

Proxy Bidding

EBay's proxy bidding system allows buyers to enter the maximum amount they're willing to pay for an item, then sit back and relax while the computer handles the bidding. It works this way: When placing a bid, bidders enter the highest amount they're willing to pay for the item. This number is kept confidential from other bidders and the seller until the auction ends. The eBay system places bids on behalf of the bidder, using only as much of the bid as is necessary to maintain the high-bid position or to meet the seller's reserve price. The system will bid up to the bidder's maximum amount.

If another bidder has a higher maximum, the first bidder will be outbid and will receive an outbid notice. At that point, a bidder can go back and rebid or choose to let the item go.

In reserve price auctions, if a bidder's maximum bid is the first to be greater than the seller's reserve price, the eBay system automatically makes a bid that meets the reserve, and the bidding process continues from there.

The drawback for sellers is that even though someone may be willing to pay more for an item, the proxy bidding system will only take the bid up to the next increment required to win the auction. But it's a benefit to buyers, because it means bidders often end up paying less than their maximum price.

Proxy bidding does not apply to multiple item (Dutch) auctions.

High-Dollar Bids

When placing a bid of $15,000 or more on eBay, users are required to provide a valid credit card or go through eBay's ID verification process. This assures sellers that the bidder is of legal age and serious about completing the transaction.

Bid Retractions

All bids on eBay are binding except those involving the sale of real estate or businesses (which fall under eBay's nonbinding bid policy) and the sale of items that are prohibited by law or by eBay's user agreement.

Though eBay rarely allows users to retract their bids, there are some circumstances when it is permitted. Whether you are selling or buying, it's important to understand the rules about bid retractions.

One such situation would be if the bidder accidentally enters the wrong amount— for example, if a bidder enters $550 instead of $55. In that case, the bidder must re-enter the correct bid amount immediately after making the retraction. If the bidder doesn't place another bid, he is in violation of eBay's policy and may face suspension.

A bid can also be retracted if the description of the item being auctioned is changed significantly after the bid is made but before the auction closes. Bids can also be retracted if the buyer cannot reach the seller by phone or e-mail (for example, if the seller's phone number on file with eBay doesn't work or if e-mail messages are returned as undeliverable).

Bids placed before the final 12 hours of a listing may be retracted if they meet one of the above circumstances but only if the retraction is made prior to the final 12 hours of the auction. A bidder who retracts a bid under these circumstances eliminates all bids he has placed on that item, so if the retraction is to correct a bidding error, a new bid must be placed.

Bright Idea

If your item is unique, specialized, or requires buyer research, use a 10-day auction so bidders have plenty of time to check it out and decide how much to bid.

For bids placed during the final 12 hours of a listing, retractions must be made within one hour of placing the bid and are allowed only if the situation meets eBay's rules. If a retraction is made within the last 12 hours, only that particular bid will be eliminated; bids placed prior to the last 12 hours will remain valid.

Of course, bidders may contact the seller and request that a bid be canceled, and the seller may honor the request or not at his own discretion.

Every user's feedback profile displays the total number of bid retractions that user has made in the past six months. Be cautious about accepting bids from a user who has a habit of retracting them. Also, eBay investigates bid retractions, and users who abuse this feature may be suspended.

It's important to note that there is no equivalent for a bid retraction in Buy It Now listings. Once a purchase has been confirmed, the buyer is obligated to pay.

Sniping

Sniping is the process of placing bids in the closing minutes or seconds of an auction. Snipers do this to avoid bidding wars that escalate the bids to more than they want to pay. Bidders can protect themselves against snipers by bidding the absolute maximum amount they are willing to pay with eBay's proxy bidding system. A sniper—or any other bidder—can only win the auction if they are willing to spend more than anyone

Let the Bidding Begin

The bid increment, or amount by which a bid is raised each time the previous bid is topped, is predetermined based on the current high bid. However, it's possible for a bidder to be outbid by less than a full increment. This would happen when the winning bidder's maximum bid beats the next highest bid by an amount less than the full increment. EBay bid increments are:

Current Price	Bid Increment
$ .01-.99	$.05
$1.00-4.99	$.25
$5.00-24.99	$.50
$25.00-99.99	$1.00
$100.00-249.99	$2.00
$250.00-499.99	$5.00
$500.00-999.99	$10.00
$1,000.00-2,499.99	$25.00
$2,500.00-4,999.99	$50.00
$5,000.00 and up	$100.00

else who has bid. When a last-second bid isn't high enough, that person rarely has time to get back in and place a winning bid before the auction ends.

A Picture Really Is Worth 1,000 Words

EBay automatically adds the camera icon to listings with pictures so someone browsing through search results knows when they click on your listing they'll be able to see what the product looks like.

While any picture is better—albeit only slightly—than no picture at all, a quality picture will make a tremendous difference in the success of your auctions. Quality photos not only let bidders see what your product really looks like, but they also say that you're a serious, professional eBay seller. Antiques seller Sue Rudolph says you'll get more and higher bids on items when your pictures are good.

Use the following tips to produce quality photos that will increase bidding on your auctions:

- Create a photo area in your home or shop with a background screen and good lighting. Cluttered backgrounds detract from your product and brand you as an amateur. Poor lighting will prevent prospective bidders from seeing the detail they need to make a decision about if and how much to bid. Schultz has an area in his office that he uses as a photo studio for his children's furniture products. "We set up foam core walls and build a little room setting, take the pictures, clean them up digitally, and put them out on eBay," he says.
- For small items, a sheet of plain poster board makes a good neutral backdrop.
- Consider developing a photo background that helps brand your business. It could be a distinctive (but not distracting) color, it may have a subtle pattern, or it could include your logo or company name.
- If appropriate, showcase your item with accessories to display it to its best advantage. Accessories should not distract from or hide any details of your products. Also, be sure to indicate whether or not those accessories are included in the auction, available separately, or not for sale.
- If you sell clothing or jewelry, invest in used mannequins to properly display them. A box draped with a piece of plain fabric works as a display pedestal.
- Take pictures from multiple angles and use more than one with your auction to showcase your product completely. In addition to a front view, consider pictures from the side and top, as well as closeups of special details.

Garriss says photography is one of the biggest cost issues for most eBay sellers. He recommends maintaining a database of pictures so it's easy to pull up images for listings when you are selling items you've sold before. "We have a library of about 350,000 images that we are able to tap when we have the same items come through again," he says.

Most eBay sellers find the investment in a digital camera worthwhile, but it needs to be a quality camera. Moran started out using print film that he would have transferred to a disk when it was processed, but that, he says, took too long. So he bought an inexpensive digital camera, and that provided pictures he could upload immediately, but the quality was poor. Then he received a higher-quality digital camera as a gift, so now he is able to take clear pictures that showcase his items well.

Beware!

As a seller, you may cancel the bid of any user with whom you feel uncomfortable completing a transaction.

If you have a scanner, you can use print film and then scan your photos. Or, if you have an image of the product from a catalog, you can scan that instead of staging a new photo—just take care not to violate any copyright restrictions.

And remember: If you're in the market for a good digital camera and/or a scanner, shop on eBay first.

Relist Me

If an item doesn't sell the first time you list it, try relisting it with a lower minimum bid. If it sells the second time around, you'll be credited for the insertion fee for the second listing. (Of course, if it doesn't sell the second time, you'll pay the fees for both listings.)

EBay makes this relisting offer under the following conditions:

○ You did not receive any bids if your listing was a regular, no-reserve auction; or, if your listing was a reserve price auction, you did not get any bids that met or exceeded your reserve price.

○ You are relisting the same item within 30 days of the closing date of the first listing.

○ You have the same or lower starting price than the first listing for a no-reserve auction, or for a reserve price auction, you relist with the same or lower reserve amount.

EBay allows one relisting per item; check eBay's policies for complete instructions and restrictions on this offer. When you relist, consider creating a different title, changing the starting price, enhancing your description, or changing or adding photos.

EBay Stores
An Easy Way to
Sell Online

Along with putting merchandise up for auction on eBay, you may want to consider opening an eBay store, which would allow you to sell your fixed-price and auction items from a unique destination on eBay. EBay stores make it easy to cross-sell your inventory and build repeat business.

▲

If your goal is a small, part-time operation selling just a few items a month, an eBay store might be helpful, but not necessary. However, if you want to build a substantial, profitable business, you may want to consider opening an eBay store. It's an excellent tool.

How do you make the decision? According to eBay, you should open an eBay store if you want all your listings displayed in one customizable place; if you want to be able to easily generate repeat business and encourage multiple purchases from the same buyers; if you want to control what you cross-sell to your customers; and if you want to maintain a larger permanent inventory than you sell through auctions.

EBay stores offer a convenient selling platform for all your eBay listings—auctions, fixed-price items, and store inventory. EBay promotes stores in several ways. All your auction listings will contain the eBay store icon; when bidders click on that icon, they are taken to your store. That icon is also attached to your eBay user ID for

Level with Me

Eay offers three store levels: basic, featured, and anchor. All have their own customizable storefront and the ability to list store inventory, but featured and anchor stores include additional services. Check the eBay Web site for current store subscription fees. Here's how the three levels differ from one another:

○ *Basic.* Your store is automatically listed in the eBay stores Directory and will appear in every category directory where you have items listed.

○ *Featured.* Your store rotates through a special featured section on the eBay stores home page; receives priority placement in "related stores" on search and listings pages; and is featured within the category directory pages where you have items listed. In addition, you receive monthly reports on your sales and marketplace performance.

○ *Anchor.* In addition to the services offered to featured stores, your store can be showcased with your logo within the eBay stores Directory pages and will receive premium placement in "related stores" on search and listings pages, which means your store will be placed higher on the page than the featured stores.

IEP Visions' David Schultz says in his own experience, and from talking to other eBay sellers, it is clear that—all else being equal—the more you invest in your eBay store, the more your store sales will be.

increased visibility. The eBay stores Directory is designed to promote all stores and will drive buyers to your particular store. You will also receive your own personalized eBay store Web site address that you can distribute and publicize as you wish.

The process of opening an eBay store is almost as simple as setting up your initial user ID. The only requirements are that you be a registered eBay seller and have a minimum feedback rating of 20 or be ID-verified.

Any items that you have in active listings at the time you open your store will not appear in your store. But any auctions or fixed-priced listing you post once your store is opened will automatically appear in your eBay store.

The cost of a basic eBay store is a nominal monthly fee (current rates can be found at www.ebay.com) that increases with the level of services you desire, along with additional fees for items listed and sold. Store inventory listings are less expensive than auction listings and appear for a longer time. However, those listings appear only in your store and do not come up in traditional eBay auction searches.

In addition to insertion fees, as with auctions, you also pay final-value fees when an item in a store listing sells.

Setting Up Your Store

Just as you would stock a physical store using well-thought-out arrangement of your merchandise, you want to apply the same principles to your eBay store. EBay allows you to create up to 11 custom categories for your products. Use these like aisles in a physical store, grouping like products together under a clear description to make it easy for shoppers to see what you have.

Depending on what you sell, you may decide to use product-based categories, such as clothing, home decor, glassware, electronics, etc. Or you might use a more flexible system, with categories like "sale items," "bestsellers" and "seasonal." Consider having a category for new items so people who visit your store regularly can quickly see what you've added recently. These custom categories can be changed and updated as often as you wish, which is a significant benefit to a seller whose inventory changes frequently.

Your store site should also clearly explain how you operate. Take advantage of the Store Policies page to provide a complete and professional description of your policies and procedures. Your About My Store page tells customers about your business. Use this space to establish your credentials and provide some history

Bright Idea

Successful store sellers use their auctions to drive traffic to their stores. Mention your store in your auction description and suggest that bidders visit your store for additional merchandise.

about you and your company. Buyers are more comfortable dealing with sellers who demonstrate that they know what they're doing.

Be sure to use your store to list all the items you have in your inventory that complement your active auctions, and be sure to mention your store in all your eBay listings.

Remember that good descriptions of the merchandise in your eBay store are as critical as they are in your auction listings. "You should describe it well, have a good title—the same features that you would have in your auction," says Cindy Mayer of Cindy's Collectibles.

Do You Want Fries with That?

You probably can't count how often you as a customer have been the target of up-selling efforts. Order a sandwich and drink at a fast-food restaurant, and you can bet you'll hear the familiar "Do you want fries with that?" question. Displays at the check-out counters of retail stores are designed to persuade you to purchase something you didn't realize you needed. Call the customer service department of most major companies, and you're not surprised when the rep tries to sell you an additional product or service after dealing with the original reason for your call. It's all based on the economic reality that subsequent sales to the same customer are more profitable than the first. And when customers are in a buying mood, you should take advantage of it.

Tip...

Smart Tip

Include your eBay store's URL in all e-mail communication with buyers. For example, add a standard line such as "Thank you for shopping with us. We add new products every week. Please visit us at www.ebaystores.com/ storename."

EBay's Merchandising Manager is a tool for eBay store sellers that helps you up-sell by allowing you to control which items your buyers see after they bid on or buy one of your items, or use the checkout function after a transaction has ended. You can choose different items to show on each listing. For example, if you're selling candleholders, show buyers the candles, lighters, snuffers, and wax remover. If you're selling clothing, show the accessories such as shoes, scarves, hats, and jewelry. If you're selling home decor or furnishings, show complementary pieces.

The tool works by allowing you to establish "merchandising relationships" for the items you list, and this determines which items the buyers will be shown. You determine what goes together by designating relationships for as many or as few items as you'd like. If you don't include cross-merchandise on one of your items, eBay will automatically select related items you are selling to display to your buyers.

No Need to Physically Stock Your Store

It's possible for you to carry items in your eBay store that you don't already own and will never actually take possession of. It can work this way: You find a distributor of products you want to sell. You put photographs and a description of those products on your store site. Note that you don't have to sell everything the distributor does. When an order comes in, you process the payment (retail price plus shipping) and then send the order to the distributor, who ships the product directly to your customer in a package that shows you as the shipper. The distributor bills you the wholesale price plus shipping and handling. You make a profit, the distributor makes a profit, and the customer is happy and comes back to buy more—it really is that simple.

This is what is known as drop-shipping, and it is a longstanding business practice. It's win-win: You don't have to stock inventory, handle the product, pack, ship, etc., and the distributor doesn't have to worry about retail sales.

Of course, you have to choose the right merchandise and deal with reputable distributors. Your customer will give you the credit for what goes right and hold you responsible for what goes wrong, even though the drop-shipper is doing the work. You should also expect to pay for the services the drop-shipper provides. That will usually appear as a drop-ship fee, but it may be included in the cost of the merchandise. Be sure you understand how the drop-shipper charges so you can build that expense into your pricing structure.

Avoid drop-shippers who want to charge an account setup fee or insist on a minimum monthly purchase. Be sure that they are factory-authorized wholesalers of the brands they represent, and that the goods they are shipping are brand-new, factory-warranted products. Go back and review the information in Chapter 3 about buying from wholesalers before you commit to a drop-shipping arrangement.

David Schultz of IEP Visions started out buying from manufacturers who would drop-ship for him. Because he didn't have to maintain any inventory, he was able to work from a spare bedroom. "I could just sit in my house all day, watching television, answering e-mails as they came in, and then shoot the orders over to the manufacturers," he says.

Because he had already worked in the children's furniture industry, he was familiar with the manufacturers and negotiated arrangements

> **Beware!**
> Do your research on your suppliers so you can avoid getting involved in a broker "daisy chain" (a chain of brokers who are each marking up the products). There is nothing wrong with buying from brokers or distributors, but you should always know who the actual seller is and be able to contact the seller directly, if necessary.

with those willing to drop-ship. As easy as the process sounds, however, Schultz readily admits that it had some flaws. As his business grew, so did the amount of shipping damage. The manufacturers were blaming the carriers, and the carriers were saying the manufacturers weren't adequately packing the items and refusing to pay the claims. Ultimately, Schultz knew he had to start maintaining his own inventory and handle his own shipping for his company to survive.

Be Prepared for the Commitment

One of the challenges of brick-and-mortar retailing is the hours—usually long, going from early morning to late evening, weekdays and weekends. Physical stores need to be staffed at least from opening to closing, and usually before and after.

By contrast, your eBay store is open for business 24/7, whether you're awake or asleep. But this doesn't mean you can put up a store and then ignore it. You need to monitor your store closely, answer questions from shoppers promptly, ship merchandise on schedule and as promised, and deal with any other customer service issues that might arise as soon as possible.

If you go on vacation or are going to be away from your store for any reason, arrange for someone else to monitor the site and take care of your business.

7

EBay
Tools

Your online image is a critical element in your success on eBay. It doesn't necessarily have to be slick and high-powered, but it does have to inspire confidence in bidders. Having a professional look to your auctions and your store (if you have one) is a major part of your online image. If you've done any browsing around eBay at all (and by now, you should have),

▲

you can tell just by looking at an auction whether or not the seller is serious about his or her business. In Chapter 5, we discussed the importance of well-written, complete listings that have been carefully spell-checked and proofread. EBay offers a variety of other tools to help you enhance your auctions, as well as your other eBay activities.

About Me Page

Your About Me page is a great way to educate bidders on what you have to offer, your policies (payment terms, shipping, returns), and why they should feel comfortable buying from you. EBay provides a number of design templates to help you quickly design a sharp, professional-looking About Me page. Before you set yours up, browse around and look at others through the eyes of a prospective customer. Take the time to formulate your policies and write appealing copy that a prospective customer will read and understand.

In some ways, your About Me page is like a jazzy resume, but instead of using it as a tool with which you apply for a job, you're using it as a tool to win the confidence and trust of potential customers. Include information about yourself, such as details on your expertise in your product areas or business experience. You might also add a photo, but make it relevant to your eBay operation. It could show you at work doing something related to your business or even just be a professional-style headshot. Many successful eBay sellers include personal details on their About Me pages, such as information about their family or hobbies. While this shouldn't be the focus of your About Me page—this isn't, after all, your personal Web site—it's still true that when bidders know something about you and feel like they can relate to you, your sales will go up.

You can also include a link to your personal Web site on your About Me page; however, you cannot offer non-eBay merchandise for sale on your About Me page.

Seller's Assistant

EBay's Seller's Assistant is a service available for a monthly subscription fee that will help you create professional listings in bulk, track them, and manage customer correspondence. The service provides easy-to-use templates for auction and eBay stores listings, and will also automatically insert your payment terms, tax, shipping, and any other details you want to include.

Seller's Assistant includes tools to help you track items, transactions, and customers. It allows you to create standard e-mail messages—such as invoices and payment receipt and shipping notifications—to make your customer correspondence faster and more accurate.

Turbo Lister

Turbo Lister is a feature-rich eBay selling tool that makes creating and posting listings in bulk faster and easier. There is no charge to use Turbo Lister, but you have to download the Turbo Lister program from eBay and install it on your computer. (Go to http://pages.ebay.com/turbo_lister/download.html, or request a CD from eBay.) The program helps you create auction listings in bulk, allows you to save listing details for items that you sell regularly so you can list them again later, saves default values for all "Sell Your Item" options to reduce data entry time, lets you duplicate items to make it easy to create listings for similar items, creates attractive item descriptions using a WYSIWYG (what you see is what you get) HTML editor, and schedules your listings to start at a specified time if you so desire.

Smart Tip

In addition to eBay's tools, consider using other auction management tools, such as the ones available from the companies listed in this book's Appendix.

Bidder-Management Tools

Certainly one of the main benefits of selling on eBay is getting your goods out there in front of millions of prospective buyers. Even so, there may be times when you want to control who can bid on your auctions. EBay offers two tools for this purpose.

The first is your blocked bidder/buyer list. This allows you to set up a list of bidders/buyers who are not allowed to bid on, or purchase, your auction listings, and it applies to all the items you have up for any type of auction. You can add to or delete from this list at any time.

This feature can be used when you have a bad experience with a bidder, such as one who doesn't pay, pays very slowly, or who is unrealistic in his or her expectations and demands, and you simply don't want to do business with that person again. EBay suggests using this feature cautiously, as it may limit the number of bids on your items.

Sue Rudolph had a bad experience with a bidder who had excessive negative feedback, so now, as her auctions near their closing time, she checks out the high bidder. If that individual has a lot of negative feedback, Rudolph sends an e-mail advising that she will not sell to that person and suggesting that he or she stop bidding on the item.

A more effective way to handle such a situation is to cancel the bid yourself and then place the bidder on your blocked bidder list. Here's how: Click on the "site map" link located at the top of most eBay pages; when that page opens, click on "Cancel bids on my item," which is located under the "Buying and Selling" heading near the top of the middle column. Follow the instructions for canceling the bid. You can also cancel a bid by going to the item's bid history page and clicking on the "cancellation" link.

Once you've canceled the bid, add the bidder to your blocked bidder list so they can't bid on any of your auctions. Be sure to cancel the bid before you add the bidder to your block bidder list, or he may end up as the high bidder even though you've blocked him from future bids. As a courtesy, send a polite e-mail to the bidder advising that you've canceled the bid and explaining your reasons.

> **Tip...**
>
> **Smart Tip**
>
> You are never obligated to accept a bid from someone you don't want to sell to. You can refuse to do business with any eBay user for any reason, but you must cancel the bid before your auction ends.

You may also create a pre-approved bidder/buyer list for any item. This allows only the people on that list to bid on or purchase your auction items. If an eBay user not on the list sees the item and tries to place a bid, she will be asked to contact you by e-mail. You can add or delete bidders from your pre-approved list up until the time the auction ends.

This is a useful tool when you want to sell something to a particular bidder but do not want to open the auction up to the public. For example, let's say you put up an item with a reserve price of $100, and the reserve was not met so the auction closed without a sale. Someone who saw the auction contacts you and offers you $95 for the item, and you decide to accept. It is against eBay policy for you to complete this transaction outside eBay. The easiest way for you to handle the situation is to relist the item with a starting bid of $95 and create a pre-approved bidder list that includes only the user ID of the bidder you have agreed to sell to.

Second-Chance Offer

Although most eBay auctions are completed without any problems, occasionally a sale doesn't go through (usually because of a nonpaying bidder). Also, sellers often have duplicate items but only put one up for auction at a time. The second-chance offer is a feature that allows sellers to offer an item to an underbidder at the underbidder's highest bid if the winning bidder does not complete the purchase or if the seller has more than one item available.

In the case of a nonpaying bidder, be sure you've done everything possible to resolve the issue before sending a second-chance offer.

As the name implies, a second-chance offer is an opportunity for the seller to sell the item (or another one like it) quickly and easily, with all the benefits of eBay's services, and without paying a listing fee. Sellers do, however, pay a final-value fee if the second-chance offer is accepted.

My eBay

My eBay is a tool that allows you to manage your buying, selling, and other account activities. Tustin, California, part-time eBay seller Linda Parker says this is her favorite eBay feature and the page she visits most on the entire eBay site because it allows her to track her auctions, what she's bidding on, her favorite sellers, and items she's just watching or searching for.

The tabs on the My eBay page are:

- *Bidding/watching.* This is the page where you track your bids, purchases, and the items you're interested in but haven't bid on (this is called watching an auction). You can create customized searches and be notified by e-mail when an item that fits your description is put up for auction on eBay. While this is

Smart Tip

Save all your auction listings in your word processing program or in your auction management software so that if you sell a similar item, you don't have to re-create the listing.

Tip...

Help! I Need Somebody!

For people who want help selling their items online, eBay created its Trading Assistant program. By the time you finish reading this book, you should be quite comfortable selling your own merchandise on eBay. And when you've gained some experience, you can make some extra money selling items for others who can't—or don't want to—do it themselves.

EBay defines Trading Assistants as "experienced eBay sellers who have indicated their willingness to sell items for others for a fee. All terms will be negotiated between Trading Assistants and their clients."

To become a Trading Assistant, you must have at least one sale within the past 30 days and a feedback rating of at least 50, with a minimum of 97 percent positive feedback. You set up a Trading Assistant profile page on eBay describing your experience, what you're willing to sell, and the services you provide. Trading Assistants typically negotiate their fees with their clients on an individual basis.

As a Trading Assistant, you are responsible for representing the product accurately in the listing and being sure it meets eBay's listing policies. Because you are listing the product, eBay considers you the seller, with all the accompanying responsibilities and obligations.

To sign up to become a Trading Assistant, go to the eBay Services page and click on "trading assistant."

obviously a benefit to buyers, Rudolph says it also comes in handy for sellers to monitor their markets and to possibly buy items they might later resell.

- *Selling.* This is the page that shows all your auction listings, sales, unsold items, and pending items (listings you've prepared but haven't launched yet).
- *Favorites.* This page lets you keep track of what's going on in your favorite categories, searches, and with other eBay sellers.
- *Accounts.* All of your eBay-related accounts are in one place.
- *Feedback.* This lets you view the feedback you've received from other users. There is also a button that takes you to a list of the transactions for which you still need to leave feedback. Charlene Davis appreciates this particular feature. "It's easy to get busy and forget to leave feedback, but feedback is a very important part of the eBay community," she says. "I periodically use this tab to see if I have any transactions that are completed that I need to leave feedback on."
- *Preferences.* This lets you control how your My eBay tool appears, how you prefer to sign in, and other eBay preferences.
- *All.* This combines all the information in all the tabs on a single page.

EBay Education

EBay offers a wide range of narrated how-to "tours" to help users learn to use the system, as well as interactive written tutorials, online seminars, and recorded events.

The eBay University program offers a range of classes held across the country that allow you to learn in a traditional setting where you can interact with instructors and other students. The program includes one-track seminars, which are a day of classes that begin in the morning with basic topics and progress to more advanced subjects in the afternoon; two-track seminars, which are an entire day of either beginner or advanced training, depending on your needs; and road show seminars, which are shorter classes taught in different neighborhoods throughout a metropolitan area over a three-day period. Additional conferences and opportunities for learning and networking are available; check the eBay site for more information.

Feedback

Feedback is the tool by which an eBay user's reputation is built. There are three types of feedback—positive, neutral, and negative—and both parties in a transaction are encouraged to leave feedback about

Bright Idea

Use your feedback profile to boost your morale when you're having a bad day. Lift your spirits by reading all the positive things people have said about you.

each other. For example, as a seller, you might leave feedback about how quickly a buyer paid; as a buyer, you might leave comments about how well the seller answered questions or how promptly the merchandise was shipped. Only the seller and the winning bidder can leave feedback about a particular transaction.

What you write in feedback becomes a permanent part of that user's record on eBay, so use caution and good judgment, especially before leaving negative comments. You cannot change feedback once it's been posted. And except under rare circumstances, eBay will not remove feedback after it is left.

> **Tip...**
>
> ## Smart Tip
>
> Andale provides counters to eBay sellers at no extra charge, and various auction management programs will also count the number of times your listing is viewed. This is a good tool to use since it lets you know how popular an item is and whether or not your auction marketing efforts are working.

An eBay user's feedback rating is the number in parentheses after his or her user ID. The feedback rating is calculated by giving one point for each positive comment, no points for a neutral comment, and subtracting one point for each negative comment. You should always check a user's profile for negative feedback, whether you're buying or selling.

Don't automatically refuse to deal with an eBay user who has a few negative feedback comments. Consider the ratio of negative feedback to positive feedback. If a user has hundreds of transactions on his or her record, don't let two negative remarks dissuade you from doing business with that person. Also, look at when the negative feedback was left—recently, or a long time ago? Read the feedback and get a sense of whether it was justified or not, or possibly retaliatory because the eBay member may have left negative feedback for that person. Many negative feedback comments sellers receive are in retaliation for negative feedback the sellers leave for nonpaying bidders. So be sure to read all negative feedback comments—and decide for yourself if they're valid.

You should leave feedback within 90 days of the completion of a transaction. Of course, the sooner, the better. As you're building your own eBay reputation, you'll gain a special appreciation for users who leave prompt feedback.

Warranty Services

If you sell electronics and computer items, you can increase your bidders' comfort level by offering a standard or extended warranty through eBay's Warranty Services program. You promote the warranty option in your listing, and a third-party company handles the warranty sale and servicing. For every warranty that is sold on one of your items, you earn a cash bonus of 25 or 50 percent of your eBay final-value fee.

▲

The general product categories for which warranties are available are computers, consumer electronics, cameras and photo, video games, and musical instruments. The item can be new, used, or refurbished, but it must be fully functional.

Due to state laws, sellers in Alaska, Guam, Maine, Oklahoma, and Puerto Rico cannot participate in the warranty program.

PowerSeller Program

EBay's PowerSeller Program is designed to recognize certain levels of achievement by eBay sellers. Because PowerSellers are held to strict standards regarding both their sales volume and their business conduct, customers are able to buy from them with confidence. In addition, PowerSellers have access to special benefits, such as the health-insurance opportunity explained in Chapter 8.

EBay's system automatically assesses users for PowerSeller eligibility and issues an e-mail invitation to join the program when a seller qualifies.

Structuring
Your Business

If your only goal with an eBay business is to periodically clear out the garage and occasionally make a few extra dollars, your business structure doesn't really matter much. But if you're using eBay to launch a substantial and sustainable operation, you need to set it up right from the beginning.

Put It in Writing

Some entrepreneurs will do just about anything to avoid sitting down and writing a business plan. Other would-be business owners get so caught up planning every detail that they never actually get their business off the ground. Ideally, you should find a happy medium between these two extremes.

Gotham City Online's Jonathan Garriss says eBay offers so many different opportunities that a written business plan is essential to help you focus. You may see 10 or more opportunities but, he says, "If you go in 10 different directions, you're not going to make a lot of progress. You [probably] don't have the resources to pursue that many opportunities. Just doing the business plan is the exercise that defines where the best opportunity is and where you are going to commit your resources."

In a perfect world, you would begin your venture with a written business plan. Writing your plans down forces you to think them through and gives you a chance to examine them for consistency and thoroughness. That's why even if you're already buying and selling on eBay and have achieved a degree of success, you need a plan.

If you're excited about your business, creating a business plan should be an exciting process. It will help you define and evaluate the overall feasibility of your concept, clarify your goals, and determine what you'll need for start-up and long-term operations.

This is a living, breathing document that will provide you with a roadmap for your company. You'll use it as a guide, referring to it regularly as you work through the start-up process and during the ongoing operation of your business. And if you're going to be seeking outside financing, either in the form of loans or investors, your business plan will be the tool that convinces funding sources of your venture's worth.

Putting together a business plan is not a linear process, although the final product may look that way. As you work through it, you'll likely find yourself jumping from equipment requirements to cash-flow forecasts to staffing, then back to cash flow, on to marketing, and back to equipment requirements. Take your time developing your plan; whether you want to start a part-time solo eBay business that never gets any larger or build a sizeable operation, you're making a serious commitment, and you shouldn't rush into it.

This book focuses on issues particular to selling on eBay, but there are additional points you need to consider when writing your plan. Read Chapter 3 in *Start-Up Basics* for complete guidelines on how to put together a general business plan.

> **Smart Tip** *Tip...*
>
> Review your business plan once a year. Check to see if you're still on track—if not, do you need to change what you're doing, change the plan, or both?

Naming Your Company

One of the most important marketing tools you will ever have is your company's name. A well-chosen name can work very hard for you; an ineffective name means you have to work much harder at marketing your company.

Your company name should very clearly identify what you do in a way that will appeal to your target market. It should be short, catchy, and memorable. It should also be easy to pronounce and spell—people who can't say your company name may buy from you, but they might not tell anyone else about you.

We asked eBay sellers how they came up with their company names. Garriss came up with the name Gotham City Online because of his New York City location. He also made sure the corresponding Web address was available before making the final decision. Adam Ginsberg says he just likes the letter Z and thought the name ZBilliards would make his company "the last word in pool tables." Cindy Hale decided to call her eBay sales operation The Walker Avenue Attic "because I live on Walker Avenue and I was selling stuff from my attic."

David Schultz's company name, IEP Visions, reflects a major mistake many online entrepreneurs make: He didn't think ahead of time about how his company was going to grow and the impact of the name on his operation. He already owned the domain name www.iepvisions.com; he had created it for a friend to use in a totally unrelated enterprise but never used it. "When we started this, I had the domain sitting around, and I just used it as a generic name, just to start out. And I basically got stuck with it," he says. Had he realized that his experiment in selling children's furniture online was going to be so successful, he probably would have considered a name that better identifies what he does. Now that he has a reputation with customers, suppliers, and the industry in general, he doesn't want to change his company's name.

Although naming your company is undoubtedly a creative process, it helps to take a systematic approach to the task. Once you've decided on a name, or perhaps two or three possibilities, take the following steps:

- *Check the name for effectiveness and functionality.* Does it quickly and easily convey what you do? Is it easy to say and spell? Is it memorable in a positive way? Ask several of your

Bright Idea

When naming your company, consider creating a word that doesn't exist—that's what companies like Exxon and Kodak did. Just be sure the syllables blend to make an ear-appealing sound and that the name is simple enough for people to remember. Also, check to make sure you haven't inadvertently come up with a name that means something with negative connotations in another language.

▲

friends and associates to serve as a focus group to help you evaluate the name's impact.

- *Search for potential conflicts.* Find out if any other business has a name so similar that yours might confuse the public.

- *Check for legal availability.* Exactly how you do this depends on the legal structure you choose. Typically, sole proprietorships and partnerships operating under a name other than that of the owner(s) are required by the county, city, or state to register their fictitious name. Even if it's not required, it's a good idea, because that means no one else can use that name. To find out how to register a fictitious name in your state, start by calling the local business licensing agency; they'll either be able to tell you or refer you to the correct agency. Corporations usually operate under their corporate name. In either case, you need to check with the appropriate regulatory agency to be sure the name you choose is available.

- *Check for use on the Internet.* If someone else is already using your name as a site on the Internet, consider coming up with something else. Even if you have no intention of developing a Web site of your own, the use could be confusing to your customers.

Learning Curve

If you understand mail order businesses, you'll have a head start with your online auction business. And if you don't, it's a good idea to learn because the two operations have a lot in common, says consultant Paul Mladjenovic. Among those similarities are that you need to find customers and build relationships without the advantage of face-to-face interaction, you need to find merchandise, and you need to create a fulfillment (shipping) system.

Mladjenovic cites two primary differences between online auctions and mail order: "The first difference is irregular inventory," he says. Mail order houses typically have a standard stock that they ship out when ordered, while online auction sellers may have less predictable resources, especially if their product line includes collectibles and used merchandise.

The second difference is the method of pricing. "Auction businesses use dynamic pricing, while mail order businesses use static pricing," says Mladjenovic. "Static pricing means, 'here is my price, buy it or don't buy it, have a nice day.' Dynamic pricing is the whole point of an auction. As bidders, potential customers set the sale price starting with whatever minimum bid you stipulate."

- *Check to see if the name conflicts with any name listed on your state's trademark register.* Your state's department of commerce can help you obtain this register or direct you to the correct agency. You should also check with the trademark register maintained by the U.S. Patent and Trademark Office (PTO). Visit the PTO Web site at www.uspto.gov for more information.

Once the name you've chosen passes these tests, you need to protect it by registering it with the appropriate state agency; again, your state's department of commerce can help you with this. Because you'll be doing business nationally, and perhaps even internationally, on eBay, you should also register the name with the PTO.

Legal Structure

One of the first decisions you'll need to make about your new business is the legal structure of your company. This is an important decision that can affect your financial liability, the amount of taxes you pay, and the degree of control you have over the company, as well as your ability to raise money, attract investors, and ultimately sell the business. However, legal structure shouldn't be confused with operating structure. The legal structure is the ownership structure (defining who owns the company). The operating structure defines who makes management decisions and runs the company.

A sole proprietorship is owned by the proprietor, a partnership is owned by the partners, and a corporation is owned by the shareholders. Sole proprietorships and partnerships can be operated however the owners choose. In a corporation, the shareholders typically elect directors, who in turn elect officers, who then employ other people to run and work in the company. But it's entirely possible for a corporation to have only one shareholder and to essentially function as a sole proprietorship. In any case, how you plan to operate the company should not be a major factor in your choice of legal structures.

So what goes into choosing a legal structure? The first point is who is making the decision on the legal structure. If you're starting the company by yourself, you don't need to take anyone else's preferences into consideration. But if there are multiple people involved, you need to consider how you're going to relate to each other in the business, as well as the issue of asset protection and limiting your financial liability in the event things don't go well.

Something else to think about is your target customers and what their perception will be of your structure. While it's not necessarily true, there is a tendency to believe that the legal form of a business has some relationship to the sophistication of the owners, with the sole proprietor as the least and the corporation as the most sophisticated. If you're going to be selling primarily to private consumers and collectors, they'll probably never know (or care) whether you're a sole proprietor or a corporation. If, on the

Beware!

Find out what type of licenses and permits are required for your business while you're still in the planning stage. You may find out that you can't legally operate the business you're envisioning, so give yourself time to make adjustments to your strategy before you've spent a lot of time and money trying to move in an impossible direction.

other hand, your target market is going to be other businesses or high-end retail buyers, it might enhance your image if you incorporate.

Your image notwithstanding, the biggest advantage of forming a corporation is in the area of asset protection, which is the process of making sure that the assets you don't want to put into the business don't stand liable for the business's debt. However, to take advantage of the protection a corporation offers, you must respect the corporation's identity. That means maintaining the corporation as a separate entity; keeping your corporate and personal funds separate, even if you are the sole shareholder; and following your state's rules regarding the holding of annual meetings and other record-keeping requirements. Do not expect a corporation to protect you personally against general liability issues, such as if someone is injured on your property or suffers an injury or damages due to your product or some other aspect of a business transaction with you. These days, lawyers sue both the corporation and the people involved, so protect yourself in that area with adequate insurance.

Is any one of these business structures better than another? No. We found eBay sellers operating as sole proprietors, partners, and corporations, and they made their choices based on what was best for their particular situation. For example, the reason Jonathan Garriss and his partner, David Topkins, chose to incorporate when they formed Gotham City Online was "planning for the future." The sole proprietors told us they simply didn't see a need to incorporate. Consider what you want to do now and where you expect to take your company, and then choose the form that is most appropriate for your particular needs.

If you decide to incorporate, do you need an attorney to set up the corporation? Again, no. There are plenty of good do-it-yourself books and kits on the market, and most of the state agencies that oversee corporations have guidelines you can use. Even so, it's always a good idea to have a lawyer at least look over your documents before you file them, just to make sure they are complete and will allow you to truly function as you want.

Finally, remember that your choice of legal structure is not an irrevocable decision, although if you're going to make a switch, it's easier to go from the simpler forms to the more sophisticated ones than the other way around. The typical pattern is to start as a sole proprietor and move up to a corporation as the business grows. But if you need the asset protection of a corporation from the beginning, start out that way. Chapter 2 in *Start-Up Basics* will tell you more about this critical part of getting started.

Licenses and Permits

Most cities and counties require business operators to obtain various licenses and permits to comply with local regulations. While you're still in the planning stages, check with your local planning and zoning department or city/county business license department to find out what licenses and permits you will need and what is involved in obtaining them. You may need some or all of the following:

- *Occupational license or permit.* This is typically required by the city (or county, if you are not within an incorporated city) for just about every business operating within its jurisdiction. License fees are essentially a tax, and the rates vary widely, based on the location and type of business. As part of the application process, the licensing bureau will check to make sure there are no zoning restrictions prohibiting you from operating in your location.

- *Fire department permit.* If your business is open to the public or in a commercial location (say your retail store has an eBay sales division, which you run onsite), you may be required to have a permit from the local fire department.

- *Sign permit.* Many cities and suburbs have sign ordinances that restrict the size, location, and sometimes the lighting and type of sign you can use in front of your business. Landlords may also impose their own restrictions. Most residential areas forbid signs altogether. To avoid costly mistakes, check regulations and secure the written approval of your landlord before you invest in a sign.

- *State licenses.* Many states require persons engaged in certain occupations to hold licenses or occupational permits. Often, these people must pass state examinations before they can conduct business. States commonly require licensing for auto mechanics, plumbers, electricians, building contractors, collection agents, insurance agents, real estate brokers, repossessors, and personal-service providers, such as doctors, nurses, barbers, cosmetologists, etc. It's unlikely that you will need a state license to sell your merchandise on eBay, but it's a good idea to check with your state's occupation licensing entity to be sure.

> **Smart Tip**
>
> When you purchase insurance on your equipment and inventory, ask what documentation the insurance company requires before you ever have to file a claim. That way, you'll be sure to maintain appropriate records, and the claims process will be easier if it is ever necessary.

Business Insurance

It takes a lot to start a business, even a small one, so protect your investment with adequate insurance. If you're homebased, don't assume your homeowner's or renter's policy covers your business equipment; chances are, it doesn't. If you're located in a commercial facility, be prepared for your landlord to require proof of certain levels of liability insurance when you sign the lease. And in either case, you need coverage for your inventory and other valuables.

A smart approach to insurance is to find an agent who works with businesses similar to yours. The agent should be willing to help you analyze your needs, evaluate what risks you're willing to accept and what risks you need to insure against, and work with you to keep your insurance costs down.

Typically, homebased business owners should make sure their equipment and inventory are covered against theft, fire, flood, and other perils, and that they have some liability protection if someone (either a customer or an employee) is injured on their property or by their product. In most cases, one of the new insurance policies designed for homebased businesses will provide sufficient coverage. Also, if you use your vehicle for business, be sure it is appropriately covered.

If you opt for a commercial location, you'll find your landlord will probably require certain levels of general liability coverage as part of the terms of your lease. You'll also want to cover your inventory, equipment, and fixtures.

Once your business is up and running, consider purchasing business-interruption insurance to replace lost revenue and cover related costs if you are ever unable to operate due to covered circumstances. For more on business insurance, read Chapter 7 of *Start-Up Basics*.

Smart Tip

Sit down with your insurance agent on an annual basis and review your insurance needs. As your company grows, it's sure to change. Also, insurance companies are always developing new products to meet the needs of the growing small-business market, and it's possible that one of these new policies will be appropriate for you.

Depending on what you sell, product liability may be an area of concern. Because he sells children's furniture, Schultz carries a substantial amount of liability insurance to protect him financially if anything goes wrong with one of his products. It makes sense that the primary issue of product liability would fall back on the manufacturer, but in today's litigious society, everybody involved in the sale of the merchandise is likely to be named in a lawsuit. Schultz recommends sitting down with an attorney and your insurance agent to analyze your potential risks and exposures, and then purchasing appropriate and adequate coverage.

In addition to property, casualty, and general liability, you may want to consider purchasing extra coverage that will pay if a claim against your basic policies exceeds their limits. This is known as an umbrella policy. Garriss says he has this type of coverage to protect his company in the event of a major catastrophe.

Professional Advisors

As a business owner, you may be the boss, but you can't be expected to know everything. You'll occasionally need to turn to professionals for information and assistance. It's a good idea to establish relationships with these professionals *before* you get into a crisis situation.

To shop for a professional-service provider, ask friends and associates for recommendations. You might also check with your local chamber of commerce or trade association for referrals. And don't overlook the Elance section of eBay.

Find someone who understands your industry and specific business, and who appears eager to work with you. Check them out with the Better Business Bureau and the appropriate state licensing agency before committing yourself to hiring them.

As an eBay seller, the professional-service providers you're likely to need include:

- *Attorney.* You need a lawyer who practices in the area of business law, is honest, and appreciates your patronage. In most parts of the United States, there are many lawyers willing to compete fiercely for the privilege of serving you. Interview several, and choose one you feel comfortable with. Be sure to clarify the attorney's fee schedule ahead of time, and get your agreement in writing. Keep in mind that good commercial lawyers don't come cheap; if you want quality

Staying Healthy with eBay

One of the biggest challenges of being self-employed or a small-business owner is finding affordable health insurance. As a service to eBay users who have achieved PowerSeller status, eBay has negotiated an agreement with a major insurance broker to provide a number of health insurance products, including major medical, dental and pharmaceutical coverage. EBay does not subsidize the cost but rather has used the size of its user base in negotiating competitive rates for its members. However, it's a good idea to compare the programs available through eBay with other options you may have before making a decision.

advice, you must be willing to pay for it. Your attorney should review all contracts, leases, letters of intent, and other legal documents before you sign them. He or she can also help you collect bad debts and establish personnel policies and procedures. Of course, if you are unsure of the legal ramifications of any situation, call your attorney immediately.

- *Accountant.* Among your outside advisors, your accountant is likely to have the greatest impact on the success or failure of your business. If you are forming a corporation, your accountant should counsel you on tax issues during start-up. On an ongoing basis, your accountant can help you organize the statistical data concerning your business, assist in charting future actions based on past performance, and advise you on your overall financial strategy regarding purchasing, capital investment, and other matters related to your business goals. A good accountant will also serve as a tax advisor, making sure you are in compliance with all applicable regulations and that you don't overpay any taxes.

- *Insurance agent.* A good independent insurance agent can assist you with all aspects of your business insurance, from general liability to employee benefits, and probably even handle your personal needs as well. Look for an agent who works with a wide range of insurers and understands your particular business. This agent should be willing to explain the details of various types of coverage, consult with you to determine the most appropriate coverage, help you understand the degree of risk you are taking, work with you in developing risk-reduction programs, and assist in expediting any claims. "Our insurance agent has been fantastic in guiding us through this process," says Garriss. "Insurance is complex, and our insurance agent is one of the professionals we have depended on for good advice on something we had no idea about."

- *Banker.* You need a business bank account and a relationship with a banker. Don't just choose the bank you've always done your personal banking with; it may not be the best bank for your business. Interview several bankers before making a decision on where to place your business. Once your account is open, maintain a relationship with the banker. Periodically sit down and review your accounts and the services you use to make sure you are getting the package most appropriate for your situation. Ask for advice if you have financial questions or problems. When you need a loan or a bank reference to provide to creditors, the relationship you've established will work in your favor.

- *Consultants.* The consulting industry is booming, and for good reason. Consultants can provide valuable, objective input on all aspects of your business. Consider hiring a business consultant to evaluate your business plan or a marketing consultant to assist you in that area. When you are ready to hire employees, a human-resources consultant may help you avoid some costly mistakes. Consulting fees vary widely, depending on the individual's experience, location, and field of expertise. If you can't afford to hire a consultant, consider hiring an MBA student from the business school at the nearest college or university.

- *Computer expert.* A computer is essential for doing business through online auctions and stores. In addition, you'll use your computer to manage your operation. Your computer and data are extremely valuable assets, so if you don't know much about computers, find someone to help you select a system and the appropriate software, and to be available to help you maintain, troubleshoot, and expand your system as needed. If you're going to have a Web site, consider hiring a professional to help you design it.

Most of the eBay sellers we talked with have ongoing relationships with accountants and know of an attorney they can call on if they need one. Many use computer consultants to assist with custom software development and Web designers to create a professional online image. Let professionals help you with the activities that are essential to the profitable functioning of your business but are not the core of your operation. That will free you up to focus on building and growing your company.

Start-Up Economics and Financial Management

There are two key sides to the issue of money: how much you need to start and operate, and how much you can expect to make. Analyzing these numbers is often extremely difficult for small-business owners who would rather be in the trenches getting the work done than bound to a desk, dealing with tiresome numbers. Because most eBay sellers get started with equipment and inventory they already own, it's easy to overlook the process of creating a sound financial plan. And if you're treating your eBay sales as a hobby that happens to generate a little extra money, it's OK if you don't do much planning. But if you want to create a real business, you need to be prepared to deal with start-up economics and ongoing financial management.

Where Will You Find Start-Up Money?

As you're putting together your financial plan, consider these sources of start-up funds:

- *Your own resources.* Do a thorough inventory of your assets. People generally have more assets than they immediately realize. This could include savings accounts, equity in real estate, retirement accounts, vehicles, recreation equipment, collections, and other investments. You may opt to sell assets for cash, or use them as collateral for a loan. Many eBay sellers auction things they already own to raise the cash they need to invest in more inventory. For example, Cindy Hale of Cindy's Collectibles generated about $2,000 selling miscellaneous items from her attic, and she used that money to invest in more inventory. Take a look, too, at your personal line of credit; most of the equipment you'll need is available through retail stores, Web sites, and eBay sellers who accept credit cards.

- *Friends and family.* The logical next step after tapping your own resources is to approach friends and relatives who believe in you and want to help you succeed. Be cautious with these arrangements, though; no matter how close you are, present yourself professionally, put everything in writing, and be sure the individuals you approach can afford to take the risk of investing in your business.

- *Partners.* Although most operations that sell on eBay are owned by just one person, you may want to consider using the "strength in numbers" principle and look for someone who may want to team up with you in your venture. You may choose someone who has financial resources and wants to work side by side with you in the business. Or you may find someone who has money to invest but no interest in doing the actual work. Be sure to create a written partnership agreement that clearly defines your respective responsibilities and obligations.

- *Government programs.* Take advantage of the abundance of local, state, and federal programs designed to support small businesses. Make your first stop the SBA; then investigate various other programs. Women, minorities, and veterans should check out niche financing possibilities designed to help these groups get into business. The business section of your local library is a good place to begin your research.

Learn more about financing a new business in Chapter 4 of *Start-Up Basics*.

How Much Do You Need?

It takes very little cash to just sell things on eBay, especially if you already have a business. However, if you purchase stock, and certainly as you grow, you'll need money to invest in inventory, facilities, and more sophisticated equipment. The eBay sellers we talked with started on eBay with very little capital and used the revenue they generated to grow their operations.

Jonathan Garriss says it took about $600 to get Gotham City Online started—that was the cost of the computer and camera he and his partner purchased on eBay. Adam Ginsberg spent nothing. He was already running a store selling billiard tables and other furniture when he began selling on eBay, so he already had the necessary computer equipment and inventory.

Tustin, California, eBay seller Linda Parker started with a computer and a digital camera—she already owned the computer, and the camera was a Valentine's Day gift from her husband. "Not very romantic, but very practical," she says. Along those lines, Cindy Mayer was happy to get a set of postal scales as her Mother's Day present one year.

The Marlers' start-up costs for their part-time eBay selling operation were zero. "We already had the equipment and owned the items," Susan says. Charlene Davis says her situation was the same. "I needed a computer, a scanner, and a camera—all of which I already owned, so there were no start-up costs."

Calculate how much you need to start your ideal business, and then figure out how much you have. If you have all the cash you need, you're fortunate. If you don't, you need to start playing with the numbers and deciding what you can do without.

The chart on page 90 gives you a list of the start-up equipment you're likely to need and the approximate cost of each item. Use it as a guide to put together your start-up budget.

> **Smart Tip** — *Tip...*
> Christmas items will sell year-round, but you'll get the best prices in October, November and December.

Pricing

In a traditional retail situation, you would buy your stock, mark it up according to a formula you felt was fair and reasonable, and put it out for sale. In an auction, the buyer determines the final selling price. Even so, you need to understand pricing so you can set your minimum bids and reserve amounts if you use them, and price the items in your eBay store.

Start-Up Expenses

Item	Price
Computer and Office Equipment and Supplies	
Computer system (with printer)	$1,700–$4,500
Digital camera	300–800
Scanner	125–600
Fax machine	100–250
Two–line full–featured phone system	70–80
Voice mail	6–20/month
E–mail	0–25/month
Web site design	500–5,000
Web site hosting	50–500/month
Uninterruptible power supply	125–250
Zip drive backup	150–300
Surge protector	15–60
Calculator	15–50
Copier	300–1,000+
Desk	200–600
Desk chair	60–200
Printer stand	50–75
File cabinet(s)	25–100
Bookcase	50–100

Start-Up Expenses, continued

Computer/copier paper	25–50
Business cards	6–12
Letterhead paper and envelopes	50–125
Address stamp	10
Extra printer cartridge	25–80
Extra fax cartridge	up to 80
Zip drive disks	45–120
Mouse pad	10–20
Miscellaneous office supplies	100–150
Storage shelves, cabinets	100–500
Shipping Equipment and Supplies	
Hand truck	55–125
High–speed tape dispenser	16–25
Carton stapler	200–500
Electronic scale	50–715
Paper shredder	25–125
Sealing tape	5–8
Boxes	225–400
Mailing labels	75–200
Cushioned mailers	150–250
Packing materials	50–350

Fun Fact

The term "dynamic pricing" is often used to describe auction pricing because the process is controlled by the bidders and is often unpredictable.

An aspect to pricing that is critical to profitable eBay selling is understanding value, says consultant Paul Mladjenovic. If you just want to clear out your garage, value is not as important as it is if you want to build a profitable business selling on eBay. But even in that case, you want to get the best price possible, and understanding value will help you do that.

A key element to consider when pricing is what similar items have sold for. You can search eBay for completed auctions and study the bid patterns and winning bids. Parker researches what similar items have sold for and sets her minimum bids lower than that figure.

In fact, many eBay sellers set their opening bid low—often as low as a dollar—and trust the market to drive up the price to a profitable level. That works for Ginsberg. "EBay is a unique marketplace," he notes. "When you put something up for $1 with no reserve, it can sell for more than if you put it up with a $1,100 reserve."

Laurie Ayers often uses the amount she paid for an item as her starting point. "I don't like to start anything below $1.99 or $2," she says. But her experience has been that setting the starting bid lower means a higher final bid price. She believes a higher starting bid may scare off bidders looking for a bargain, but a lower starting figure can generate enough interest to start a bidding war.

Cindy Mayer considers her cost as well as the market when pricing. "I'll search for completed auctions. If I can find [the same or a similar item] and see what the high and low bids were, I'll start somewhere in-between," she says. "If it's something that I had personally in my house for ten years, I consider it no cost to me, so I may start the bidding a little lower than I otherwise would. If it's something that I purchased brand-new or at a consignment shop, I usually only start about $2 over my cost, and that has been quite effective." Mayer figures she is representative of many eBay shoppers, so she tries to do what would appeal to her. "I'm not a big spender. I look for bargains, and I want to give people bargains, too."

Ginsberg lists most of his pool tables with a starting price of 1 cent and no reserve, and counts on the market to drive up the final sale price to a profitable level—and most of the time, it does. On rare occasions he takes a hit and sells a table at a loss, but his profits are sufficient to absorb those losses.

When pricing items for Gotham City Online, Garriss considers his cost and what he thinks the merchandise will sell for. "We are not in the camp of starting things at a dollar and let's see what happens," he says.

Schultz takes a similar approach. He generally sets his minimum bid within 10 percent (below or above) of his actual cost, depending on the item, with no reserve. Sometimes he takes a hit and either loses money or just breaks even, but most of the time he makes a respectable profit.

Cindy Hale doesn't lock herself in to any specific pricing formula. "I played with pricing until I found a price that would sell," she says. "The rule of thumb in the beginning was a 100 percent markup. That didn't really work well. Now, it depends on the item. Most items are marked up 50 percent, but I have a few things that I got great deals on, and the markup can be 1,000 percent."

How much profit should you make? There's no hard and fast rule or a clear definition of how much profit means you are successful. In general, however, when buying items at wholesale to sell retail, look for a gross profit of at least 15 percent.

Will you ever sell an item for less than it cost you? Probably. Will you sell an item for more than you thought it was worth? Again, probably. Just know that with experience, your pricing skills will sharpen.

How Will You Get Paid?

Most Internet shoppers want instant gratification. They want to buy something online, win an auction, pay quickly and easily, and have their merchandise on their doorstep as soon as possible. Most don't want to mail you a check and wait for it to arrive, get deposited and clear the bank before you ship their goods. And they're probably not

Taxing Matters

A potentially sticky area for online auction sellers is sales tax. Many large retailers with online operations have begun collecting sales tax on their Internet sales, and legislation affecting how Internet sales are taxed is pending at state and federal levels. As a business owner, you are responsible for knowing the law and doing the right thing. Whether or not you need to collect and remit state and local sales tax depends on a variety of factors, including your product line, where your business is located, and where your customers are. Also, many states have what's known as casual sale exemptions that might apply if you're just selling your own items in what amounts to an online garage sale.

"You need to know the rules of the state you're in," advises Chuck Norman, CPA, a partner with Ernst & Young in Toledo, Ohio. "Talk to your accountant or contact your state's revenue service, and be sure you clearly understand the rules as they apply to your business."

To charge and collect sales tax, you'll need a sales tax ID number (sometimes referred to as a reseller's permit). This is usually a very simple process; just check with your state's department of revenue for information on how to proceed.

Beware!

Mail thieves operate even in the nicest of neighborhoods. If you receive checks and money orders in the mail, rent a post office box so you know they will be secure.

thrilled about going to the hassle of buying a money order or getting a certified check. So if you're going to sell online, it's best if you can accept some type of credit card, either with your own merchant account or with one of the many online payment services available to you.

If you're planning to grow a substantial business, you really need your own merchant account. Don't be intimidated by this process. There was a time when getting a merchant account was extremely difficult and expensive. It's much easier now, but high-volume online sellers still find dealing with merchant-account providers a challenge. "This has been one of the sore points as we've grown our business," says Garriss. "You talk to the credit card company, and they think you are some fly-by-night mail order operation. I think it's a holdover from when credit card companies didn't want to offer merchant accounts to people who were doing mail order sales. It's frustrating. You just don't have any credibility [with merchant per account providers] if you are an Internet company."

Ginsberg expresses the same frustration. "That was one of our biggest problems," he says. "[Merchant service providers] give you a $25,000 per month limit. For us, that's four hours of sales." After lengthy negotiations, Ginsberg finally has his merchant-account limit at a level that meets his company's needs.

Schultz had a similar experience, which is largely why he recommends going through your own bank for a merchant account rather than using a merchant-account service company.

An alternative to getting your own merchant account is to use a service such as PayPal, which is an eBay company that allows you to accept credit cards, electronic checks, and cash payments over the Internet. While PayPal is the most popular payment service on eBay, there are others you might want to consider. See the "Payment Resources" section in this book's Appendix for a list.

Escrow Services

For higher-priced items, many buyers like to use an escrow service, which means that the winning bidder sends the payment to a neutral third party (an escrow company) to be held until the goods are shipped and the bidder is satisfied with their condition.

The benefit of escrow is that the escrow company is neutral, so both the buyer and seller are protected. Of course, you'll expect to pay for this service; the fee varies depending on the details of the transaction.

With escrow, the buyer is protected because the seller isn't paid until the merchandise is delivered and inspected. The seller is protected because he doesn't ship the goods until the escrow service verifies receipt of the funds.

Be sure the escrow company you choose is legitimate and licensed. Don't be offended if your buyers want to check out the escrow company before sending money—and when you're buying, you should do the same. Escrow scams are fairly easy to pull off, and victims have little recourse.

Credit Card Fraud

Credit card fraud is a significant problem for buyers, sellers, and credit card issuers. For card-present, in-store transactions, liability for fraud belongs to the credit card issuer. For card-not-present transactions, including online transactions, liability for fraud shifts to the seller. That means sellers don't receive payment for fraudulent online transactions. Don't let this stop you from doing business online, but take steps to limit your risk.

One of the most important fraud prevention steps you can take is to deal with established, credible, reputable merchant-account providers (the acquiring bank) and processors. Your payment-gateway provider (where authorizations and payments are processed) should offer real-time credit card authorization results to prevent charges on cards that have been reported as lost or stolen, or that are no longer valid for any other reason.

Use an address verification service that matches the cardholder billing address on file with the billing address submitted. Use card security codes, which are numbers that appear on Visa, MasterCard, and American Express cards that are never printed on receipts. The ability of a customer to provide these codes is additional assurance that the actual card is in the possession of the person conducting the transaction.

Monitor your transactions for suspicious activity. Watch for multiple orders purchased on the same credit card for items such as electronics, which are easily resold. Finally, develop a negative card and shipping address list and crosscheck orders against it. Many criminals will return to the same merchant to make fraudulent transactions.

Keeping Records

There are many reasons why you need to keep good records on your income and expenses, including the fact that you need to know whether or not you are making a profit, what particular items are more profitable than others, and how much you have to pay in taxes. Before you launch your business, set up a system that allows you to

Tip...

Smart Tip

For record-keeping, use a paper system, any one of the popular accounting software packages, or a good auction management software package.

keep complete and detailed records on everything you spend and earn.

Chuck Norman, CPA, a partner with Ernst & Young in Toledo, Ohio, advises sitting down with a competent tax advisor to be sure you understand all your responsibilities and obligations regarding local, state, and federal taxes. You also want to be sure to take every deduction to which you are entitled, and report all your income. Failing to report income on your tax return is a crime and can land you in a lot of trouble. If you have employees, you need to understand and follow the rules regarding payroll taxes. Your tax advisor can guide you on any other applicable tax issues.

You can keep your records manually or use any of the popular off-the-shelf accounting systems available today. Choose the system that's easiest for you. Read Chapters 14 through 17 of *Start-Up Basics* for details on the issues of bookkeeping, financial statements, financial management, and taxes.

Monitoring Your Financial Progress

One of the key indicators of the overall health of your business is its financial status, and it's important to monitor your financial progress closely. The only way you can do that is to keep good records. Chapter 14 in *Start-Up Basics* explains how to create and

Tax Attack

Businesses are required to pay a wide range of taxes, and there are no exceptions for companies that sell on eBay. Keep good records so you can offset your local, state, and federal income taxes with your operating expenses. If you have employees, you'll be responsible for payroll taxes. If you operate as a corporation, you'll have to pay payroll taxes for yourself; as a sole proprietor, you'll pay self-employment tax. Then there are property taxes, taxes on your equipment and inventory, fees and taxes to maintain your corporate status, your business license fee (which is really a tax), and other lesser-known taxes. Take the time to review all your tax liabilities with your accountant, and read Chapter 17 in *Start-Up Basics* for more on this important topic.

maintain a set of books. An alternative is to ask your accountant for assistance in setting up your system. The key is to do it correctly and completely from the very beginning, and keep your records current and accurate throughout the life of your company.

Keeping good records helps generate the financial statements that tell you exactly where you stand and what you need to do next. The key financial statements you need to understand and use regularly are:

- *Profit and loss statement (also called the P&L or the income statement).* This statement illustrates how much your company is making or losing over a designated period—monthly, quarterly, or annually—by subtracting expenses from your revenue to arrive at a net result, which is either a profit or a loss.

- *Balance sheet.* A balance sheet is a table showing your assets, liabilities, and capital at a specific point; a balance sheet is typically generated monthly, quarterly, or annually when the books are closed.

- *Cash flow statement.* This summarizes the operating, investing, and financing activities of your business as they relate to the inflow and outflow of cash; as with the profit and loss statement, a cash flow statement is prepared to reflect a specific accounting period, such as monthly, quarterly, or annually.

Successful eBay sellers review these reports regularly, at least monthly, so they always know where they stand and can quickly move to correct minor difficulties before they become major financial problems. Read Chapter 15 in *Start-Up Basics* for more on this subject.

Beware!

Report your income from eBay sales on your tax return no matter how insignificant you think it is. Remember that failing to report income is a crime. Also, be sure to take any deductions to which you are entitled.

Locating and Setting Up Your Business

The flexibility of selling on eBay gives you a lot of choices as to where to locate your operation and how to get it set up. You can opt for a retail store or a warehouse location, or you can work from home.

Because of the room required to store inventory and handle shipping, homebased eBay sellers will find their growth limited by the space they have available. Whether or not this is a problem for you depends on your own personal goals. If you are looking to create a sizable company with several employees and generate hundreds of thousands of dollars each year in sales, there's no question about it—you'll need a commercial location. But if your goal is a small business that generates a comfortable income for you, being homebased may be the ideal situation. A variety of other business goals and situations fall between those two extremes, so think about what your goals are, and then consider your various location options.

The Home Advantage

The decision to set up your business at home will depend on a number of things, including local zoning codes, your landlord (if you have one), your family situation, your budget, and your own plans for how you want to operate your company.

A particular challenge to operating a homebased eBay business is that it can take up a lot of room. You'll need a place to set up your desk and computer, an area for staging product photographs, an area for packing and shipping tasks, and storage for your inventory and supplies.

Ideally, you should have a section of your home you can set aside for exclusive business use, but that's not always practical or possible. Tustin, California, eBay seller Linda Parker has her desk and computer in one room, with her inventory stored on a high shelf that runs the perimeter of her kitchen—"that keeps breakables away from my two-year-old's dangerous hands," she says— and her packing and shipping area in the garage.

Cindy Mayer's eBay operation is more physically focused. "We have a finished basement, with a room off it that is not finished. Now it's finished with eBay things." Cindy Hale has her eBay operation set up in a workshop behind her house. "I have about 300 square feet dedicated to my items. We built bay shelving that reaches the ceiling, and I can keep a fair amount of inventory in there," she says.

The most obvious advantage of being homebased, especially in the beginning, is the small initial capital outlay. The money you might otherwise have spent on leasing commercial space can be invested in your inventory or on marketing and promotional expenses.

A homebased business also offers substantial tax breaks, but you must be sure your setup meets IRS requirements. According to *The Ernst & Young Tax Guide* (John Wiley & Sons), the IRS says that certain expenses are deductible if part of your home is "your principal place of business for any trade or business in which you engage, or [it is] a place to meet or deal with your patients, clients, or customers in the normal course of your trade or business." But you must choose a room—and to take the home office deduction, it must not be just a corner of a room—to use solely as your office and/or workroom. If it also contains a TV or stereo and serves as a den or guest room, or if you work on the dining room table, your home office deduction probably will not hold up under an IRS audit. For example, Parker's setup likely wouldn't qualify, but Mayer's and Hale's would.

What can you deduct? Directly related expenses, which are those that benefit only the business part of your home, and a portion of indirect expenses, which are the costs involved in keeping up and running your entire home. For example, your office furniture and equipment are fully deductible as directly related expenses. In the area of indirect expenses, you may deduct a portion of your household utilities and services (electric, gas, water, sewage, trash collection, etc.) based on the percentage of space you use for business purposes. Other examples of indirect expenses include real estate taxes, deductible mortgage interest, casualty losses, rent, insurance, repairs, security systems, and depreciation.

Before you invest too much time in planning or setting up a homebased operation, check your local zoning codes and any deed restrictions that may be attached to the property. Many municipalities have ordinances that limit the nature and volume of commercial activities that can occur in residential areas. Some outright prohibit the establishment of homebased businesses. Others may allow such enterprises but place restrictions regarding issues such as signage, traffic, employees, commercially marked vehicles, and noise. Find out what, if any, ordinances are in place regarding homebased businesses before applying for your business license; you may need to adjust your plan to be in compliance. Call your city hall's general information number and ask to be referred to the appropriate department—usually the planning and zoning department, or perhaps the business and occupational licensing office. Don't ask the clerk for advice; instead, get a copy of any ordinances concerning homebased businesses and the specific zoning code that applies to your property. You may need to consult an attorney who can interpret the fine points of the ordinance. Also, there is often a substantial difference between what an ordinance says and the way it is enforced.

If your business will violate the zoning code, you may still be able to operate by applying for a variance or conditional-use permit. Or you can apply to have the zoning changed. Both these processes are lengthy and require a significant amount of documentation, so you should seriously consider everything involved before you begin the process.

Smart Tip

Tip...

Even if your homebased office setup does not meet IRS requirements that would allow you to deduct those expenses, you can still deduct other expenses—inventory, storage, equipment, shipping, automobile, marketing, etc.—that are legitimate costs of doing business.

Going Retail

You have a number of options if you decide to open a retail store, and what you choose depends on the products you're selling. Understand that the face-to-face retail side of your operation will be very different from your eBay side. With that in mind, some of the factors you need to consider when deciding on a retail location for your business are:

- *Anticipated sales volume.* How will the location contribute to your sales volume? Consider the presence or potential presence of other businesses that will compete with you, and be sure the market is strong enough to support all of you.

- *Accessibility to potential customers.* Consider how easy it will be for customers to get to your business. If vehicle traffic on the street where you'll be located is often heavy, or if the speed limit is more than 35 mph, drivers may have difficulty entering or leaving your site. Narrow entrances and exits, turns that are hard to negotiate, and parking lots that are always full are deterrents that can prevent would-be customers from patronizing your shop. If you are relying on strong pedestrian traffic, consider whether or not nearby businesses will generate foot traffic for you. Large department stores will draw many customers, and shopping centers in busy office districts might attract pedestrian shoppers, particularly during weekday lunch hours. By contrast, a strip center anchored by a supermarket may not be the best location; grocery shoppers rarely browse through a strip mall either before or after they do their food buying. Consider the entrance to the site. Is it on the street level or an upper floor? Can it be reached from a main street, or is it difficult to find? Take some time to analyze the site. Monitor foot and auto traffic patterns at different times of the day. See if those patterns fit the hours you want to do business. Visit the prospective site on several different days to assess any changes in the pattern.

- *Rent-paying capacity of your business.* The best locations will usually command the highest rents. If you've done a sales and profit projection for your first year of operation, you will know approximately how much revenue you can expect to generate, and you can use that information to decide how much rent you can afford to pay. Chapters 15 and 16 in *Start-Up Basics* explain how to create and use cash flow worksheets to help with your financial management plans.

- *Restrictive ordinances.* You may encounter unusually restrictive ordinances that make an otherwise strong site less than ideal, such as limitations on the hours of the day when trucks can legally load or unload. Cities and towns are composed of areas—from a few blocks to many acres in size—zoned only for commercial, industrial, or residential development. Each zone may have its own restrictions. A commercial zone may permit one type of business but not another, so check the zoning codes of any potential location before pursuing a specific site or spending a lot of time and money on a market survey.

- *Traffic density.* Modern site analysis distinguishes between automobile and pedestrian traffic. If auto traffic were the only type of traffic important to a profitable operation, most businesses would be located near highways or main roads. Given that so many successful businesses are located on side streets away from busy roads, you clearly need to consider pedestrian traffic as well. With careful examination of foot traffic, you can determine the approximate sales potential of each pedestrian passing a given location. Two factors are especially important in this analysis: total pedestrian traffic during business hours and the percentage of that traffic that's likely to enter your shop.

- *Customer parking facilities.* The site should provide convenient and adequate parking, as well as easy access for customers. Storefront parking is always better than a rear lot; people like to be able to see the parking lot before they turn off the main thoroughfare. The lot should be well-lit and secure. Consider whether the parking area will need expansion, resurfacing or striping—possibly at an additional cost to you. If you're looking at a freestanding location, think big and envision how you will accommodate the hordes of customers your business will eventually attract.

- *Proximity to other businesses.* Neighboring businesses may influence your store's volume, and their presence can work for you or against you. Studies of the natural clustering of businesses show that certain types of companies do well when located close to one another. For example, men's and women's apparel and variety stores are commonly located near department stores. Restaurants, barbershops and candy, tobacco, and jewelry stores are often found near theaters. Florists are often grouped with shoe stores and women's clothing stores.

- *History of the site.* Find out the recent history of each site under consideration before you make a final selection. Who were the previous tenants, and why are they no longer there? There are sites—in malls and shopping centers, as well as in freestanding locations—that have been occupied by successions of

Combo Deal

Choosing your location doesn't have to be a mutually exclusive exercise. If you like working at home but still need retail space or commercial storage, simply operate from more than one location. Ginsberg, for example, has two 8,000-square-foot warehouses where his pool tables are received, customized, and repacked for shipping out. He and his customer service staff of three work in an office located in the basement of his home.

business failures. The reasons for the failures may be completely unrelated to the success potential of your operation, or they could mean your business will meet the same fate. You need to study and understand why previous tenants failed so you can avoid repeating their mistakes.

- *Terms of the lease.* Be sure you understand all the details of the lease because it's possible that an excellent site may

> **Bright Idea**
> Hang wall clocks set to different time zones in your office. You'll be able to see at a glance what time it is where your customers are, rather than having to do the calculation in your head before you place a call or leave a message.

have unacceptable leasing terms. The time to negotiate terms is before you sign the lease; don't wait until you've moved in to try to change the terms.

- *Rent-advertising relationship.* You may need to account for up to six months of advertising and promotion expenditures in your working capital. Few businesses can succeed without any sales promotion, and the larger the sum you can afford for well-placed, well-targeted advertising and promotions, the greater your chances of success. The amount you plan to spend on advertising may be closely related to your site choice and the proposed rent. If you locate in a shopping center or mall supported by huge ad budgets and the presence of large, popular chain and department stores, you will most likely generate revenue from the first day you open your doors—with no individual advertising at all. Of course, your rent will be proportionately higher than that of an independent location. If you don't locate in an area that attracts a lot of foot traffic, you will experience a slower growth rate, even if your business fronts a high-traffic street. Your real profits will come as you develop a customer base—and this will require advertising and promotion. Both center developers and tenants recommend that operators just starting out begin in small community centers and then graduate to larger regional centers or malls.

Nonretail Commercial

If you don't want to—or simply don't have the room to—operate from home, but you don't want to build a retail business, consider leasing space in a warehouse or light industrial facility.

If your inventory includes temperature-sensitive items, be sure the facility is adequately air conditioned. Also, thoroughly research security and accessibility issues, especially if you expect to be working late at night or on weekends.

When David Schultz started IEP Visions, he worked in a spare bedroom at home, and that was fine as long as he was using drop-shippers and never had to handle the merchandise. As his company grew, he needed more space. He now has 17,000 square feet in an office/light industrial park in Orlando, Florida. About 1,000 square feet is office space, plus a small showroom area where he sets up assembled products to photograph them. The remainder is warehouse space that houses inventory ranging in value from $250,000 to $400,000 at any given time.

> **Tip...**
>
> **Smart Tip**
>
> When looking for stock to buy, watch for great deals from sellers who have lost their storage space or who don't have room to store everything they have. When circumstances force someone to sell quickly, the buyer usually benefits.

Equipping Your
eBay Business

Most eBay sellers start their businesses with equipment they already own, and you'll probably do the same. That's what makes selling on eBay such an attractive business proposition. Even though you can get started with just your computer and either a digital camera or scanner, there are lots of other pieces of equipment that range from helpful to

▲

essential, depending on your particular operation. You don't need every single piece of equipment listed in this chapter to get started, but you should consider each one and decide how it works in relation to your own goals and growth strategy.

Basic Office Equipment

Many entrepreneurs find a trip to the local office supply and equipment store more exciting than an excursion to any mall. It's easy to get carried away when you're surrounded with an abundance of clever gadgets, all designed to make your working life easier and more fun. But if, like most new business owners, you're starting on a budget, discipline yourself and buy only what you need. Consider these basic items:

- *Typewriter.* You may think that most typewriters are in museums these days, but they actually remain quite useful to businesses that deal frequently with preprinted and multipart forms, such as order forms and shipping documents. The determination of whether or not you need a typewriter is one only you can make based on your specific operation. A good electric typewriter can be purchased for $100 to $150.

- *Computer and printer.* A computer is absolutely essential if you're going to be selling on eBay. In addition, it can help you manage complex bookkeeping and inventory control tasks, maintain customer records, and produce marketing materials. At a minimum, you'll need a computer with a Pentium-class processor, the most current version of Windows, 64MB RAM, an 8GB to 10GB hard drive (or larger), a CD-ROM drive, a 56 Kbps modem, and a video card.

- *Software.* Think of software as your computer's "brains"—the instructions that tell your computer how to accomplish the functions you need. There are many programs on the market that will handle your accounting, inventory, customer-information management, and other administrative requirements. Software can be a significant investment, so do a careful analysis of your own needs, and then study the market and examine a variety of products before making a final decision.

- *Modem.* Modems are necessary to access online services and the Internet, and have become a standard component of most computers. Depending on your own needs and preferences, you'll have to decide whether you want a basic telephone line modem (which probably comes standard with your computer), a cable modem (about $200 for the hardware and $100 to install), a DSL modem ($150 to $500), or an ISDN modem (about $250 for the hardware and $200 for setup). Serious eBay sellers don't have time to wait for a telephone dial-up modem to upload photos or browse Web pages at a leisurely pace; consider investing in DSL or a cable modem for quicker, more efficient operations.

- *Data and equipment protection.* You need an uninterruptible power supply to keep your computer from going down in the event of a power failure or brownout, as well as a surge protector to protect your system from power surges. You can buy these items separately or as a combined unit. You'll also need a data backup system that allows you to copy the information from your computer to another location for safe storage. For more about purchasing a computer, printer, software and peripherals, read Chapter 8 in *Start-Up Basics.*

- *Photocopier.* The photocopier is a fixture of the modern office and can be very useful to even the smallest business. At the least, it will come in handy when you have to copy documentation in the event you have a damage claim with a shipping company. The larger your operation, the more likely you are to need to make photocopies of a variety of things. You can get a basic, low-end, no-frills personal copier for less than $400 in just about any office supply store. More elaborate models increase proportionately in price. If you anticipate a heavy copy volume, consider leasing a photocopier.

- *Fax machine.* Most eBay sellers communicate by e-mail or phone and rarely need to send documents by fax. As with a photocopier, the larger your operation, the greater the chance that you'll need fax capabilities. If or when you do, you can either add a fax card to your computer or buy a stand-alone machine. If you use your computer, it must be on to send or receive faxes, and the transmission may interrupt other work. For many businesses, a stand-alone machine on a dedicated telephone line is a wise investment. Expect to pay $100 to $250 for a fax machine.

- *Postage scale.* A postage scale is a valuable investment for eBay sellers. An accurate scale takes the guesswork out of postage and will quickly pay for itself. It's a good idea to weigh every piece of mail—both envelopes and packages—to eliminate the risk of items being returned for insufficient postage, or overpaying if you are unsure of the weight. Mechanical scales typically range from $10 to $25 and will be sufficient as you are getting started. As your sales volume increases, you'll want a digital scale, which is somewhat more expensive—generally from $50 to $200—but significantly more accurate than a mechanical unit. Or you

Beware!
Though integrated, multifunction devices—such as a copier/printer/fax machine or a fax/telephone/answering machine—may cost less to acquire and take up less space in your office, but you risk losing all these functions simultaneously if the equipment fails. Also, consider your anticipated volume of use with the machine's efficiency rating and cost to operate, and compare that to stand-alone machines before making a final decision.

may want to invest in an electronic computing scale that weighs the item and then calculates the rate via the carrier of your choice, making it easy for you to make price and service comparisons. Programmable electronic scales range in price from $80 to $250.

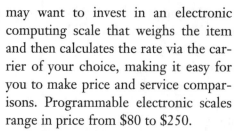

Dollar Stretcher

When looking to buy equipment for your business, always shop on eBay as well as on other Web sites, warehouse stores, chain stores, and other suppliers before making a final purchase decision.

- *Postage meter.* Postage meters allow you to pay for postage in advance and print the exact amount on the mailing piece when it is used. Meters also provide a "big company" a professional image, are more convenient than stamps, and can save you money in a number of ways. Postage meters are leased, not sold, with rates starting at about $30 per month. They require a license, which is available from your local post office. Only four manufacturers are licensed by the U.S. Postal Service to manufacture and lease postage meters; your local post office can provide you with contact information. Smaller eBay sellers find that buying postage online is an affordable and convenient alternative to leasing a postage meter.

- *Paper shredder.* A response to both a growing concern for privacy and the need to recycle and conserve space in landfills, shredders are becoming increasingly common in both homes and offices. They allow you to efficiently destroy incoming unsolicited direct mail, as well as sensitive internal documents before they are discarded. Shredded paper can be compacted much tighter than paper tossed in a wastebasket, and it can also be used as packing material. Light-duty shredders start at about $25, and heavier-capacity shredders run from $150 to $500.

Telecommunications

Advancing technology gives you a wide range of telecommunications options. Most telephone companies have created departments dedicated to small and home-based businesses; contact your local telephone service provider and ask to speak with someone who can review your needs and help you put together a service and equipment package that will work for you. Specific elements to keep in mind include:

- *Telephone.* Whether you are homebased or in a commercial location, two telephone lines should be adequate. Your telephone itself can be a tremendous productivity tool, and most of the models on the market today are rich in features you will find useful. Such features include automatic redial, which redials the last number called at regular intervals until the call is completed; programmable memory for storing frequently called numbers; and a speakerphone for hands-free use. You may also want call forwarding—which allows you to forward calls to another number when you're not at your desk—and call waiting, which signals you that another call is coming in while you are on the phone. These services are typically available through your telephone company for a monthly fee. If you're going to be spending a great deal of time on the phone, consider a headset for comfort and efficiency. A cordless phone lets you move around freely while talking, but these units vary widely in price and quality, so research them thoroughly before making a purchase. You'll pay $70 to $150 for a two-line speakerphone with a variety of standard features necessary for a business.

- *Answering machine/voice mail.* Because your business phone should never go unanswered, you need some sort of reliable answering device to take calls when you can't do it yourself. Whether you buy an answering machine (expect to pay $40 to $150 for one that is suitable for a business) or use the voice-mail service provided through your telephone company (anywhere from $6 to $20 per month) is a choice you must make depending on your personal preferences, work style, and needs.

- *Cellular phone.* Once considered a luxury, cellular phones have become standard equipment not only for businesspeople, but for just about everyone. Most have features similar to your office phone—such as caller ID, call waiting, and voice mail—and equipment and service packages are very reasonably priced. Features such as digital images, text messaging, e-mail, news services, and more are becoming increasingly available and affordable. Cell phones are especially convenient for eBay sellers who spend a lot of time shopping at garage sales, flea markets, and thrift shops for their inventory.

- *Toll-free number.* You may want to consider providing your customers with a toll-free number so they can reach you without having to make a long-distance call. Most long-distance service providers offer toll-free numbers and have a wide range of service and price packages. Shop around to find the best deal for you.

- *E-mail.* E-mail allows for fast, efficient, 24-hour communication, and it's an essential tool for eBay sellers. Consider setting up a separate e-mail address for your eBay selling activities to help you manage your business correspondence more effectively. Check your messages regularly and reply to them promptly.

Dollar Stretcher

Save money by recycling boxes and packaging materials. Whenever you receive shipments, whether items you purchased personally or inventory and supplies for your business, save the packing materials to use again.

▲

Other Equipment

In addition to these basics, there are other items you may need, depending on your particular operation. They include:

- *Digital camera.* Besides your computer, the most important piece of equipment for an eBay seller is a digital camera. Yes, you can use a traditional film camera, but that means you spend time and money on processing, and then you have to scan the picture before you can put up the auction. And if your pictures don't turn out well, you have to shoot them again and wait for them to be developed before launching your auction. Be sure to get a good-quality digital camera, one that will show the detail of your products. There are many digital cameras on the market, and new technologies are being introduced regularly. If you don't know much about digital cameras, use the discussion board feature in eBay's "Community" section to get input from other users about which camera brands and models work well and which ones don't.

- *Scanner.* Even if you have a digital camera, a scanner can be useful. Sometimes you'll have manufacturer's photos of a product that you can scan in and use, instead of—or in addition to—your own pictures. If you are selling two-dimensional items, such as trading cards and photographs, you can use a scanner to create the image that will accompany your auction listing.

- *Cash register.* If you have a retail operation, you need a way to track sales, collect money, and make change. You can do this with something as simple as a divided cash drawer and a printing calculator, or you can purchase a sophisticated, state-of-the-art point-of-sale system that is networked with your computer. Of course, the latter will cost somewhere between $1,200 and $5,000 per terminal and may not be a practical investment for a small start-up operation. A preferable option is an electronic cash register (ECR), which can range from $600 to $3,000 and can be purchased outright, leased, or acquired under a lease-purchase agreement. The newer ECRs offer such options as payment records to designate whether a customer paid by cash, check, or charge; department price groupings (appropriate for stores with multiple departments so you can separate the prices for items in each department); sign-in keys to help you monitor cashiers and clerks; and product price groups (which let you organize

Bright Idea

If you have employees, get their input when making purchasing decisions on supplies and equipment. The people who are using these items every day know best what works and what doesn't, what is efficient and what isn't.

products as they are rung up) for tracking inventory more effectively.

- *Credit and debit card processing equipment.* This could range from a simple imprint machine to an online terminal. Credit and debit card service providers are widely available, so shop around to understand the service options, fees, and equipment costs. Expect to pay about $500 for a "swipe" machine that reads the magnetic strip on cards. You'll also pay a transaction charge, which might be a flat rate (perhaps 20 to 30 cents) per transaction or a percentage (typically 1.6 to 3.5 percent) of the sale. You'll probably pay higher transaction fees for Internet sales, because the fraud risk the bank is accepting is higher than with face-to-face transactions. We examined credit card options in Chapter 9, and Chapter 5 in *Start-Up Basics* discusses more about accepting credit and debit cards.

Dollar Stretcher

Just about any type of second-hand business equipment can be purchased for a fraction of its original retail cost. In addition to shopping on eBay for used items, check the classified section of your local newspaper and ask new-equipment dealers if they have trade-ins or repossessions for sale. Careful shopping for pre-owned items can save you hundreds of dollars.

Use the "Equipment and Supplies Shopping List" on page 117 to make sure you've considered every item you may need for your business. Remember, if you're on a budget, start small and acquire equipment and supplies as you grow. This may take some serious discipline on your part, especially in the beginning, but it will be worth it in the long run.

Vehicles

The largest single piece of equipment you'll need is a vehicle to take packages going out of the area to shipping companies such as the post office or UPS, and for shopping expeditions. You need a reliable, fuel-efficient vehicle with sufficient cargo capacity. Some eBay sellers drive vans; others have found that smaller cars with fold-down backseats and hatchbacks are sufficient and easier to maneuver.

If the vehicle you presently own is suitable, using it—at least during the start-up process—will conserve your initial capital outlay. If it's not, or if you prefer to maintain a personal vehicle and a business vehicle, you'll have to lease or purchase one that will meet your needs. When you're ready to buy a vehicle, check eBay Motors before making a final decision.

Security

Whether you are homebased or in a retail or commercial warehouse location, remember that small merchandise, office equipment, and cash attract burglars, robbers, and shoplifters. Not only do you need to protect your inventory and equipment with alarms, lighting, and a careful selection of employees, but you also need to secure your personal safety as well as that of your employees.

> ### Bright Idea
> If your storage space is limited, try negotiating a deal like this with your suppliers: Make a long-term purchase commitment to earn volume pricing, but arrange for delivery in increments so you don't have to store the goods.

Begin by investigating your area's crime history to determine what kind of measures you need to take. To learn whether your proposed or existing location has a high crime rate, check with the local police department's community relations department or crime prevention officer. Most will gladly provide free information on safeguarding your business and will often even personally visit your site to discuss specific crime prevention strategies. Many also offer training seminars for small businesses and their employees on workplace safety and crime prevention.

Common techniques retailers use to enhance security and reduce shoplifting include mirrors, alarms, and video monitors. Technology is bringing the cost of these items down rapidly, and installing them may also earn you discounts on your insurance premiums. You can also increase the effectiveness of your security system by discreetly posting signs in your store windows and around the store announcing the presence of the equipment.

Purchasing

No matter how smart a consumer you are, when it comes to business purchasing, you're playing a new game. The rules are different, and the stakes are significantly higher. But correctly done, purchasing—or procurement—will increase your net income.

Choosing Suppliers

Whether you're buying items for your inventory, a major piece of office equipment, or a toner cartridge for your laser printer, you should evaluate each vendor on quality, service, and price. Look at the product itself, as well as the supplemental services and support the company provides. And always check eBay before you make a final buying decision. "We always check eBay first, and we find some pretty good deals there," says Gotham City Online's Jonathan Garriss.

Verify the company's claims before making a purchase commitment. Ask for references and do a credit check on the vendor just as you would on a new customer. A credit check will tell you how well the supplier pays his own suppliers. This is particularly important for inventory sources because it could ultimately affect you. If your vendor is not paying his own vendors, he may have trouble getting materials, and that may delay delivery on your order(s). Or he may simply go out of business without any advance notice, leaving you in the lurch. Also confirm the company's general reputation and financial stability by calling the Better Business Bureau, any appropriate licensing agencies, trade associations, and D&B.

Sign on the Dotted Line

Contracts are an excellent tool to make sure both supplier and customer are clear on the details of the sale. Garriss says that one of his early mistakes that became a significant learning experience involved failing to get an adequate contract with a vendor. This is not "just a formality" that can be brushed aside. Read all agreements and support documents carefully, and consider having them reviewed by an attorney. Make sure everything that's important to you is in writing. Remember, if it's not part of the contract, it's not part of the deal—no matter what the other person says. And if it's in the contract, it's probably enforceable—even if the other person says that never happens.

Any contract the vendor writes is naturally going to favor the vendor, but you don't have to agree to all the standard "boilerplate" terms. In addition, you can demand the inclusion of details that are appropriate to your specific situation. Consider these points when you're negotiating contracts:

- *Make standard provisions apply to both parties.* If, for example, the contract exempts the vendor from specific liabilities, request that the language be revised to exempt you, too.
- *Use precise language.* It's difficult to enforce vague language, so be specific. A clause that states the vendor is not responsible for failures due to "causes beyond the vendor's control" leaves a lot of room for interpretation; more precise language forces a greater level of accountability.
- *Include a "vendor default" provision.* The vendor's contract probably describes the circumstances under which you would be considered to be in default; include the same protection for yourself.
- *Be wary of vendor representatives who have to get any contract changes approved by "corporate" or some other higher authority.* This is a negotiating technique that generally works against the customer. Insist that the vendor invest personnel with authority to negotiate.

<table>
<tr><td>

Dollar Stretcher

Ask suppliers if payment terms can be a part of your price negotiation. For example, can you get a discount for paying cash in advance?

</td></tr>
</table>

A major component of the purchasing process is the supplier's representative, or salesperson. The knowledge and sophistication level of individual salespeople often depends on the product or industry; however, they can be a tremendous source of education and information. Some businesspeople dismiss sales reps with an attitude of "I don't have time to see peddlers," but this is a mistake. Make it a rule to treat all salespeople with courtesy and respect, but insist that they do the same for you. You can, for example, set and enforce a policy that salespeople are seen only by appointment, or at certain hours. You can also ask them in advance how much time you need to allot for your meeting, and stick to that schedule.

Besides telling you what they have, salespeople should also be asking questions. A good salesperson will try to find out what your needs are and how his or her company can satisfy them. Just as in the consumer sales arena, commercial salespeople use both high- and low-pressure tactics. Consider studying sales techniques so you can recognize and respond to the methods being used on you.

Build Strong Supplier Relationships

Reliable suppliers are an asset to your business. They can bail you out when you make an ordering mistake, or when your clients make difficult demands on you. But they will do so only as long as your business is profitable to them. Suppliers, like you, are in business to make money. If you argue over every invoice, ask them to shave prices on everything they sell you, or fail to pay your bills promptly, don't be surprised when their salespeople stop calling on you or refuse to help you when you're in a bind.

Of course, you want the best deal you can get on a consistent basis from your suppliers—this is just good business. Just keep in mind that no worthwhile business arrangement can continue for long unless something of value is rendered and received by all involved. The best approach is to treat your suppliers the way you would like each of your customers to treat you.

Find out in advance what your suppliers' credit policies are and pay according to their terms. Most will accept credit cards but will not put you on an open account until they've had a chance to run a credit check on you. They may ask you to provide a financial statement; if they do, don't even think of inflating your numbers to cover a lack of references. This is a felony, and it's easily detected by most credit managers.

If you do open an account with a supplier, be sure you understand their terms and preserve your credit score by paying on time. Typically, you'll have 30 days to pay, but many companies offer a discount if you pay early.

Equipment and Supplies Shopping List

Use the following checklist as a shopping guide to get your workspace and store (if you start a retail operation) set up. Each item listed is not necessarily required before you start, but you may want to have most of them eventually.

Computer and Office Equipment and Supplies

❏Computer system (with printer)
❏Digital camera
❏Scanner
❏Fax machine
❏Two-line, full-featured phone system
❏Voice mail
❏E-mail
❏Web site design
❏Web site hosting
❏Uninterruptible power supply
❏Zip drive backup
❏Surge protector
❏Calculator
❏Copier
❏Desk
❏Desk chair
❏Printer stand
❏File cabinet(s)
❏Bookcase
❏Computer/copier paper
❏Business cards
❏Letterhead paper and envelopes
❏Address stamp or labels
❏Extra printer cartridge
❏Extra fax cartridge
❏Zip drive disks
❏Mouse pad
❏Miscellaneous office supplies

Storage Fixtures and Hardware

❏Storage shelves, cabinets

Store Equipment/Fixtures and Supplies (for retail operations)

❏Special displays, related hardware
❏Display shelving
❏Cash register
❏Counter
❏Price marking equipment
❏Floor gondolas
❏Pegboard
❏Hooks
❏Showcases
❏Wall gondolas

Retail Supplies

❏Cash register tape
❏Shopping bags
❏Gift boxes
❏Sales tags and/or labels

Shipping Equipment and Supplies

❏Hand truck
❏High-speed tape dispenser
❏Carton stapler
❏Postage scale
❏Paper shredder
❏Sealing tape
❏Boxes
❏Mailing labels
❏Cushioned mailers
❏Packing materials

Other Equipment

❏Company vehicle
❏Signage
❏Security system

Customer
Service

Do you sometimes—or even often—feel that good customer service is a thing of the past? It may be in some business environments, but eBay is a different story. EBay customers demand—and enjoy—a high level of customer service, and if you're going to succeed at selling on eBay, you need to take care of your buyers. "Customer service is your number-one priority," says children's furniture seller David Schultz of IEP Visions. "The eBay buyer is out there looking for a great deal." Most of them know what they're looking for and have a good sense of its value, and they expect good service as part of the bargain.

We asked eBay sellers what's different about customer service when you're selling on eBay as opposed to through other channels.

"It's much more intensive," says Gotham City Online's Jonathan Garriss. "[Bidders] ask a lot more questions, and there is a lot more hand-holding." Also, he notes that the procedures for completing a transaction (payment method, shipping issues, etc.) vary significantly among eBay sellers, "so you have to work very hard to convey your message of what to do next, and how to complete the order."

An aspect unique to online auctions is the feedback system (discussed in Chapter 7), where both buyers and sellers can leave comments about one another that are visible to all other eBay users. Providing poor customer service puts you at risk of negative feedback, which could have a serious impact on your sales. While most eBay users are reasonable and honest with the way they use the feedback system, a few see it more as a weapon than a tool. Adam Ginsberg of ZBilliards calls this attitude "legalized extortion"—even when the customer is being unreasonable or is just plain in the wrong, they sometimes threaten to leave negative feedback to get what they want.

Thank You

for your purchase from OurPreciousKids. I hope you are pleased with your item. If there are no problems, please leave positive feedback for me on eBay. That way, I will know you received your purchase. If you have concerns, please contact me at Lauriepa@attbi.com. Thanks again—it was a pleasure working with you.

www.LaurieAyers.com

"Try to work with difficult customers as best you can," advises Cindy Hale, but, she adds, "Don't let nasty customers threaten you with negative feedback. Do exactly what you say you are going to do. When I first started, some buyers tried to intimidate me by saying they would leave me negative feedback. I'm way past that these days. I just tell them, 'I have done everything I can do and everything I promised to do in my auction to make you happy, and it has become apparent to me that I cannot please you. I said I would do [whatever it was]. The offer is good until [a certain date]. Please tell me if you

Smart Tip — Tip...

As soon as you get your first bid on an item, get it packaged and weighed so you're ready to send it out as soon as the auction closes. Then, once you've received payment, insert your inside label, packing slip or other documents, seal the package, affix the shipping label, and it's ready to go.

accept. If that isn't good enough, then you are certainly free to say whatever you choose to say about me in feedback. I have no control over what you say.'" If a buyer leaves you negative feedback, the eBay system allows you to post a response to it.

Some customers are difficult because that's their basic nature, but others may give you a hard time simply because they don't know any better. Garriss says it's important to keep in mind that eBay is one of the easiest ways to buy something on the Internet, which means it attracts a lot of novice online shoppers. "But if you've never done an online transaction before, you get a little concerned, a little nervous," he notes. That's why communication immediately following the close of an auction and then throughout the remainder of the time it takes to process the sale is critical.

David Schultz of IEP Visions recommends not taking it personally when customers are rude and excessively demanding. Many of his children's furniture customers are pregnant, often with their first child, and that makes them understandably anxious if anything goes wrong with their order. "New mothers want to make sure that everything is perfect, and it's our job to make sure that everything is perfect for them," he says. "You've got to understand what you are dealing with, and don't take it personally. Just fix the problem."

Communication Is Key

As soon as an auction closes, send the winning bidder a notice that outlines how the transaction will proceed. If you need to calculate the shipping before they pay, do so promptly. Let them know when you receive their payment and when you plan to ship. Once you have shipped, let them know the package is on the way and provide tracking information if available. Tell them when you post feedback, and ask them to post feedback for you when they have received the product. If you don't hear from them after they've had time to examine the item, follow up with an e-mail asking if they are satisfied. If they leave you positive feedback, thank them, and tell them you hope to do business with them again.

From the minute you post an auction, be prepared to respond to e-mails promptly. Remember, these are messages coming from potential customers or existing customers who may purchase again. Schultz says you should expect to receive and answer an average of two e-mails for each auction you put up. When you fail to answer a question in a timely manner, you have probably lost a bid.

"I can't tell you how many times I've been shopping for something and saw an auction that interested me, but I wanted more information about the item before I placed

---

Seller, Protect Thyself

EBay offers the following tips for sellers to assure smooth, problem-free transactions:

- ○ Represent your merchandise fairly and accurately.
- ○ Respond promptly to buyer questions.
- ○ Review buyer feedback so you know something about the person you're selling to.
- ○ Include a clearly stated return policy in your listing.
- ○ Ship with a tracking number and insurance to help resolve disputes if a customer claims nondelivery or if an item is damaged in transit.
- ○ Keep your shipping receipts so you have proof of shipment.
- ○ Only ship items to the buyer's verified billing address.
- ○ Don't ship until you have verified payment, which means holding merchandise until checks clear.
- ○ Keep copies of any proof you have of your item's authenticity.
- ○ Use extra caution with international payments, revised shipping information, unknown or new buyers, and unusual bidding activity on an item.
- ○ Contact your buyer immediately after an auction ends to thank them for the purchase, provide any final pricing and payment information, and let them know how long you will wait for payment and when you will be shipping the merchandise after payment is received.
- ○ If you want to limit the bidders you will accept, be sure to clearly state that in your auction description. For example, you might say, "No bidders with negative feedback" or "New bidders with no feedback must contact the seller before bidding."

a bid," says Charlene Davis. "It's great when the seller answers promptly. When they don't, I don't bid and—who knows?—I might have been willing to pay more than the highest bidder if my question had been answered."

If you see a pattern in the types of questions you get asked, look for ways to answer them in your item description or on your About Me page. You can also develop standard responses that you can easily paste into an e-mail and quickly customize for the particular situation.

Treat all your communications with other eBay users as business correspondence, and remember that the structure, tone, and details of your e-mails are a strong reflection of your operation. Begin your e-mails with a salutation, write in complete sentences, end with a proper closing, and proofread and spell-check; then proofread again before you hit "send."

Davis shares a story that emphasizes the importance of proofreading, not just running spell-check. With PayPal, sellers can opt to accept credit cards, which involves an extra fee, or to only accept cash payments through the system, which is free. She was interested in bidding on an item with payment terms of "cash, e-checks, check, or

---

Dear Buyer...

Whether you use auction management software or create your own systems, automation is a key to success when selling on eBay. Cindy Hale developed her own standard e-mail messages that she sends customers. Below is the fill-in-the-blank e-mail she sends to buyers when an auction closes:

Congratulations! You are the winner of my auction for the _____, eBay auction number 123456789. Your total with shipping is as follows:

Item:	$20.00
Shipping with delivery confirmation:	$12.60
Grand total:	*$32.60*

I accept money orders, PayPal and checks. I only accept checks if your feedback rating is 50+. How did you want to pay for that?
Looking forward to your reply!
Sincerely,
Cindy Hale

---

money orders," but the listing also mentioned PayPal. Davis wanted to use a credit card through PayPal, so she e-mailed the seller and asked if he accepted PayPal. He replied: "Yes, PayPal is a great way to pay, just with a credit card."

Davis bid on the item, won the auction and paid as she planned, with a credit card through PayPal. The payment was immediately declined, and she received an e-mail from the seller that said, "Sorry, but I do not accept credit card payments. The fees are too much. This was explained on the auction site and again in the payment e-mail."

Davis went back to the original e-mail and sent it to the seller. He had left out one single word—"not"—which meant his message said the exact opposite of what he meant. "He meant to write that PayPal was fine, just *not* with a credit card," Davis says. "I ended up mailing him a personal check, but it was a hassle. It would have been so much easier if he had proofread his e-mail before he sent it."

Providing Great Customer Service

Whether your business consists exclusively of auctions, or you also sell from a Web site or even a brick-and-mortar store, the basic principles of customer service remain the same:

- *See your business through your customers' eyes.* Is your operation user-friendly, efficient, and responsive? With their questions and high expectations, Garriss says eBay customers will force you to thoroughly understand your business processes.

- *Ask what your customers want and need.* Don't assume that you know what your customers want; ask them—and listen to their answers.

- *Meet or exceed expectations.* When you promise to do something—whether it's provide information, ship a product, or something else—do as you promised, or better.

- *Ask if there's anything else you can do.* When the transaction is complete, find out if you can provide any other product or service. A simple, "Is there anything else I can help you with?" can net you additional sales and invaluable goodwill.

- *Keep in touch.* Let your customers know that they are important to you after the sale is complete and you've gotten their money.

- *Be a copycat.* Pay attention to good customer service when you receive it, whether it's in a restaurant, the grocery store or elsewhere, and duplicate those techniques in your own operation.

Dealing with Nonpaying Bidders

When it comes to nonpaying bidders, give your customers the benefit of the doubt, at least in the beginning. Your auction listing should clearly state your payment terms. Typically, sellers ask that payment be made within three to ten days of the close of the auction, and most bidders do that because they're excited about their purchase and eager to receive the merchandise. When your auction closes, send the bidder an invoice with the final amount due (including shipping, handling, insurance, and any other charges that may apply) that clearly states when payment is due. You can do this through eBay, with your auction management software, or manually via e-mail.

If you have not received payment by the due date, send a follow-up notice—but be nice about it. You can create your own notice, or use the standard payment reminder notice eBay provides (you'll see a button for that on the "Items I've Sold" section of your My eBay page). Consultant Paul Mladjenovic tells the story of winning an auction on eBay, but between the time he placed the winning bid and the time the auction closed, his mother was rushed to the hospital and spent several days in intensive care. He understandably forgot about making the payment. On the fourth day, he says, he received a nasty e-mail from the seller. He explained his situation to the seller and paid for the item promptly, and the seller apologized for the tone of the follow-up e-mail. Clearly, it would have been better all the way around had the seller's follow-up note been a gentle reminder with a request for communication if there was a reason for payment not being made.

Of course, you will encounter bidders who are unable to pay or who change their minds after winning a bid and decide to default on the auction contract. Rudolph recalls being strung along for weeks by a buyer who kept asking for a little more time

Dishing the Dirt

When a New Jersey police officer purchased wireless speakers that a Canadian eBay seller advertised as "brand-new" but which arrived dirty and clearly not new, he had trouble reaching a resolution with the seller. He was also frustrated that eBay's feedback system only allowed him 80 characters to tell his story. So Stephen Klink created www.ebayersthatsuck.com as a place for people who believe they have been scammed on eBay to tell their stories and warn others. When he sent the link to the seller, he received a refund for the speakers.

In addition to complaints, the site offers a place for frequent eBay users to appear on a list of "good eBayers" for a small monthly fee.

to pay for an item. She never paid, and Rudolph ended up having to relist the item and file for a credit on her final-value fee for the completed auction item that was never paid for. This is the type of bidder you'll want to put on your blocked bidder list (explained in Chapter 7).

When a bidder doesn't pay in the amount of time you stipulate in your terms and does not respond to payment reminders, you are free to relist the item and sell it to someone else. You should also file a nonpaying bidder alert and request a credit on your final value fee for that transaction. You may file a nonpaying bidder alert at least seven days but no more than 45 days after your auction closes. To file a nonpaying bidder alert, go to "Help," search for "nonpaying bidder," and follow the instructions.

Establish a Return and Refund Policy

Decide how you're going to deal with returns, and state that policy clearly in all your auctions. If your return policy requires in-depth explanation, provide this on your About Me page.

Sample Return Policy

The following is a sample return policy and may give you a few ideas on how you might want to word yours:

We want our customers to be happy, which is why we provide a 30-day, no-questions-asked, money-back guarantee on all products. If for any reason you are not satisfied with your purchase, notify us by e-mail or phone, and we will promptly issue a Return Merchandise Authorization (RMA). Any item listed as "all sales final" will not be accepted for return, and no refund or credit will be issued. Shipping charges are not refundable unless the return is due to our error.

To assist us in expediting your return, exchange and/or refund, we ask that you:

❑ Contact us prior to returning the merchandise.

❑ Return the merchandise to us within 30 days of the date you received it.

❑ Return products in their original packaging in resaleable condition.

❑ Include all accessories.

❑ Include a copy of the invoice and/or packing slip.

❑ Mark the RMA number clearly on the outside of the box so we can easily identify your package when it arrives and handle your return promptly.

Refunds are made in the same form as your payment and will be issued within seven days of our receipt of the returned merchandise. If your payment was made by personal check, your refund will be held until we can confirm that your check has cleared. You may elect to receive credit instead of a refund.

Beware!
Although eBay makes every effort to protect its users from fraud, it is not totally impossible for a hacker to penetrate the system (whether eBay or another auction site) and steal personal financial information. Be cautious when revealing your information, and check your bank and credit card statements carefully.

Your return policy should include a time limit, a description of the circumstances under which items can be returned, who pays for shipping (Will you refund shipping costs if an item is returned? Most sellers don't.), whether or not you charge a restocking fee, and any procedures customers must follow to return an item. If your return policy promises to make refunds to dissatisfied customers, you are required by federal law to do that.

"I've had to issue refunds a few times, but it doesn't happen often," says Laurie Ayers. "I'm not going to argue with people too much. If they are not happy, they can send it back and I'll issue a refund." She will also consider a partial refund if the customer isn't totally satisfied but is willing to keep the merchandise.

Being reasonable, even when the customer is in the wrong, can pay off. Part-time eBay seller Susan Marler auctioned a Sprint Nokia cell phone, and the winning bidder wanted to send the phone back because she thought it would work with her AT&T service provider, but it didn't. Though Marler would have been within her rights to refuse to accept the return because she had described it accurately and the bidder made the error, she says, "I agreed to let her send it back and give her a refund, minus shipping paid. She thought about it and decided to keep it and sell it herself on eBay."

Problems with Your Drop-Shipper

If you are selling new products purchased through a distributor who drop-ships for you, and something arrives with a factory defect or damage, it is the distributor's responsibility to handle the problem. However, your customer didn't buy from the distributor; he bought from you. So you need to stay involved until the situation is resolved.

You should already know your distributor's return policy, so when you find out about a defective product (and for Internet sales, that news will usually come via e-mail), you should simply follow the steps your distributor requires. Typically, you'll contact the distributor, explain the problem, get a return merchandise authorization, and ask them to arrange to have the product picked up. Then you'll e-mail your customer with the RMA number and instructions for the return (such as repackaging the product in the original box, writing the RMA number on the outside of the box, and coordinating the pickup). Your distributor should also replace the defective product at no additional charge to you or your customer.

SquareTrade

SquareTrade is a great eBay tool to reduce the risk of problems with transactions. By displaying the SquareTrade seal on your auctions, you are demonstrating a level of trustworthiness, and buyers will feel confident that they will have a positive experience dealing with you. For a small monthly fee, SquareTrade offers buyer protection services, negative feedback notification, dispute resolution, and more. For additional information, check out eBay's SquareTrade section by clicking on the "Services" link at the top of eBay's home page, and then clicking on "Buying & Selling."

Bright Idea
Treat your customers like gold—because they are!

Common Auction Scams

While it's not specifically a customer service issue, you should still understand the common scams that occur in the auction world, be able to recognize them, and know what to do if you believe it's happening in one of your auctions. Though eBay works hard to maintain the integrity of the auction process, unscrupulous people will always try to circumvent the rules to increase their profits. All the following scams are against eBay policies.

Bid Shielding

Bid shielding is when someone uses a secondary user ID or has another eBay member bid on an item to raise the bidding to an extremely high level, and then that high bid is retracted at the last minute, and the low bid level of another bidder is protected. An example would look like this: Mary puts a necklace and earring set up for auction; the set is reasonably worth $35. Susan bids $20 and then asks Kathy to bid $50 to scare away other bidders. Kathy places her bid but at the last minute retracts it. Because no one else has bid, Susan gets the jewelry at her bid of $20. EBay's proxy bidding system and policies on bid retractions make bid shielding difficult, but enterprising scammers will still try to do it.

Shill Bidding

Shill bidding has plagued legitimate auctions since they began in ancient Rome. In a traditional auction, a person known as a shill will place bids to drive up the price of an item and then back off and let another bidder win the auction when the price is sufficiently high. The same thing can happen in an online auction; someone places bids to artificially raise the price of an item.

EBay users might participate in shill bidding, either in an effort to generate interest in their own auction or to help a friend. Don't do this type of insincere bidding; it could result in being suspended from eBay. To avoid even the appearance of being involved in shill bidding, eBay recommends that family members, friends, and individuals who live together, work together, or share a computer not bid on each other's items. Even though eBay benefits from shill bidding because higher sale prices mean higher final-value fees, buyers will be reluctant to bid if they suspect shill bidding, and that is ultimately not good for eBay as a company as well as the entire online auction community.

In addition to being against eBay's policies, shill bidding is illegal in many jurisdictions and can result in criminal prosecution.

False Testimonials

Some sellers have been known to create fake user IDs so they can place glowing testimonials about themselves in the feedback section of eBay and in the comment section of other auction sites. In addition to being unethical, this is fraudulent.

The Value of Repeat Business

In an ideal world, every sale would be equally profitable. But you're not going to be selling in an ideal world, and you need to recognize that for most companies, subsequent sales are generally more profitable than the initial sale, which is why you should have a system in place to encourage repeat business.

"We make it as easy and as safe for people to shop with us on eBay as we possibly can," says Jonathan Garriss. Gotham City Online features great pictures, thorough product descriptions, and a liberal return policy. The company accepts virtually all forms of payment. "People get very comfortable with us, and it results in repeat customers and great word-of-mouth publicity. It's very beneficial for your business."

Cindy Mayer says good service generates repeat business for her—quality merchandise, careful packing, and prompt shipping all bring customers back. She also offers a discount on the winning bidder's next eBay purchase to encourage repeat business.

"The single toughest thing to do in the world of business is to get a customer the first time around," says consultant Paul Mladjenovic. Once you've got that customer—by answering e-mails promptly, providing a quality product and great customer service, following up as necessary and appropriate, etc.—take advantage of the fact that they know you and trust you, and sell to them again.

> **Bright Idea**
>
> A great customer service technique that will also help increase sales in your eBay store is to offer free or discounted shipping on items a winning bidder might purchase from your store on the same day the auction they win closes.

13

Inventory, Storage, and Shipping

Now we're ready to tackle some more of the nuts and bolts of running an eBay business: inventory, storage, and shipping.

Inventory and Storage

Regardless of the size of your operation, accurate inventory maintenance and tracking is critical. You need to know what's on order, what's on its way to you, what you have on hand, and what's been shipped. Small part-time eBay sellers can do that manually, sometimes even by just doing a quick visual check of the area where they store their inventory. But if you're going to grow, you need a system, and the best and easiest time to put that system in place is when you're getting started.

A companion issue to tracking your inventory is how and where you store it. Storage is a key issue for eBay sellers. If you have adequate storage space, you can buy at great prices off-season and sell when those items will go for the greatest profits. If your storage space is limited, you'll have to be more selective about what you maintain in inventory.

Another issue to consider about storage is the quality of the environment. Is it air conditioned? Dry? Free of odors (especially cigarette smoke, but even household and pet odors) that might be absorbed by your merchandise?

Sue Rudolph stores her inventory in a specially outfitted closet in her computer room. As a part-time seller, when she wants to list something, she just opens the closet, studies her inventory, and makes a selection.

Though still small, Laurie Ayers is a higher-volume seller. She has shelving units in her office marked "to be listed," "listed," and "closed, waiting payment." She moves items from one area to the next as appropriate. "I try to send things out the day I receive payment, so I don't have a 'paid, to be shipped' shelf," she says.

Cindy Mayer has a separate room for storing inventory and preparing items for shipping. Items are stored on shelves according to category, and clothing is washed, pressed, and hung up for easy access. She has one shelf designated for items that are currently being auctioned and another for items that have closed and are awaiting payment and shipping.

In The Walker Avenue Attic, Cindy Hale uses a card system she developed herself. For each item in inventory, she creates an index card with all the pertinent information about the item (what it cost, what it sold for, listing fees, etc.). The cards are maintained in an inventory file while the merchandise is on hand and up for sale. When an item sells, she moves the card to a sold file while she waits for payment. When payment is received and the item is shipped, she adds all the necessary final information to the card and moves it to a complete file. "I tried Excel spreadsheets and fancy

> ## Smart Tip
> *Tip...*
>
> Keeping unsold inventory on hand is expensive and a waste of space. If something hasn't sold in a reasonable time—Laurie Ayers will give it two chances in an auction—get rid of it.

inventory software, but this is a better fit for my little business," she says.

Clearly, it's possible to earn a respectable income selling on eBay and using manual inventory management methods. But if you're going to build a business based on technology (selling on the Internet), why not go all the way and use technology to track and maintain your inventory?

Bright Idea

Offer customers a choice in shipping methods: basic, low-cost ground, plus same-day, next-day, or second-day air service if they need the item in a hurry and are willing to pay for that privilege.

"Probably the most important aspect of having an online business is being able to manage your inventory in a nonmanual way," says Jonathan Garriss. At any given time, Gotham City Online has thousands of items in inventory, all tracked by a sophisticated, customized system.

Garriss recalls talking to an eBay shoe seller who typically stocks anywhere from 500 to 600 pairs of shoes at a time and tracks her inventory with yellow sticky notes. He says she spends an average of six hours a day writing those notes and trying to find items. Inventory management software could cut that to literally minutes. Another point to keep in mind is that many auction management software programs and services include an inventory management element.

If you're selling collectibles, used items, merchandise you pick up at garage sales, etc., you will have to maintain and track those items in your inventory. However, if you're going to buy wholesale to resell, you have two options: You can buy in large quantities and store the goods until you sell them, or you can buy from distributors who will drop-ship your merchandise to your customers, and you can avoid the hassle of maintaining any inventory. We discussed the drop-shipping process in Chapter 6 as it relates to stocking your eBay store; it can also work well with auctions, other types of Internet sales, and mail order.

Shipping

In most eBay transactions, the buyer pays for shipping, but that doesn't mean you don't have to worry about handling this part of the transaction effectively and efficiently. Because shipping can add substantially to the bottom-line cost of an item for bidders, many eBay sellers focus on products that are small, easy to pack, and don't cost a lot to ship.

Linda Parker set up a packing and shipping station in the garage of her Tustin, California, home to make this part of eBay selling faster and more efficient. Other home-based eBay sellers have taken similar steps, realizing that spending an excessive amount of time on packing and shipping has a negative impact on your overall profit picture.

▲

Many eBay sellers say one of their biggest early mistakes was underestimating shipping charges. If you are setting a fixed shipping price in your auction (which is more and more difficult to do fairly and accurately, since rates vary so much according to the package's destination), be sure you calculate it accurately. Susan Marler sold an item for $8 plus shipping. But the shipping cost she estimated in her auction was $4 less than what it actually turned out to be, which seriously eroded her profit on the sale. Many sellers are now asking buyers to e-mail them their address when the auction ends so that they can calculate exact shipping charges to that address instead of setting a fixed, ballpark shipping cost in each auction. Although it's sometimes more work to do it this way (the seller has to calculate exact shipping charges on each and every package), buyers often appreciate knowing that they aren't paying more than what it actually costs the seller to ship the item to them. A decent postage scale is essential so you can quote accurate shipping charges. See Chapter 11 for more on scales.

If you choose to set fixed shipping prices, when you're writing your auction description, go ahead and weigh the item while you have it out and in your hands. Then add a pound or so (depending on how large and/or fragile it is) for packing

---

It's All in the Technique

Some items require special packing attention, such as:

○ *Artwork.* Use cartons specially designed for artwork, and use generous amounts of bubble wrap and cushioning material. Items that are of very high value or are particularly awkward in shape should be professionally packed or crated. Remove glass from framed artwork and pack separately.

○ *High-value coins, stamps, and jewelry.* In addition to packing to protect the contents, use larger-than-necessary boxes to reduce the risk of the package being lost or stolen.

○ *China and glassware.* Double-box whenever practical. All pieces should be individually wrapped in clean paper or tissues. Add a two- to three-inch layer of crumpled paper or other cushioning between the items and inner wall of the carton. Cups, dishes, saucers, and shallow bowls should be placed in the carton on edge. Deep bowls, glasses, and serving vessels should be placed in the carton with their rims toward the bottom of the carton. Fill the center of hollow items, such as vases, with paper to make them more solid.

○ *Electronics.* When shipping televisions, computers, stereo systems, and other electronic devices, use the original cartons and packing, if possible. If not, use antistatic bubble wrap and lots of cushioning materials.

---

materials. It's also reasonable to add a small charge to cover the cost of your packing materials. However, be fair with your shipping and handling charges. Certainly cover your costs, but resist the urge to make this a profit center. Experienced buyers will recognize that you're trying to make a profit on the shipping part of the sale, and they might not buy from you because of it.

"People don't mind paying a little more for shipping when the item is fragile and you're going to the time and expense of packing it well and double-boxing it," says Rudolph.

Bright Idea

Before you put your first item up for auction on eBay, understand what you need to do to ship it safely—what packing materials you need, what carriers can handle it, and anything else that will enable you to get the merchandise on the way to your customers promptly. Also, make sure you have—or can easily obtain—the appropriate-size box.

While that may be true, Paul Mladjenovic tells of the time he bought a CD for $1.99. "I confess that I didn't read the entire listing, and that would have made a difference. But I really wanted the information, and the organization that sent it to me charged me $12 for shipping, handling, and insurance." The CD arrived in a simple envelope with a postage stamp, and Mladjenovic felt he had been seriously gouged by the seller.

"Are there times when you can reasonably charge more than the price of the item for shipping and handling? Yes. If I'm selling a brick and you're buying it for $1, it's going to cost a lot more than that to ship it. But people understand that," Mladjenovic says. "So you've got to put [all the shipping-related costs] into the description. Otherwise, people might feel they were cheated. And on eBay, if [someone feels like you have cheated them], they are going to put a negative feedback rating in place, and that's your reputation."

When calculating shipping charges, be sure to keep the density of your item in mind. Very light, bulky items are likely to be subject to dimensional weight charges—that is, you have to pay for the space your shipment is taking up rather than the weight. Carriers use a standard formula to calculate dimensional weight based on the measurements of the package, and you pay based on the actual weight or the dimensional weight, whichever is more.

You might be tempted to add value to what you're selling by stressing in your auction that the shipping price includes the cost of your shipping materials. Cindy Hale says don't bother. "Customers don't care what you have to do to ship something" or how many packing peanuts you have to use, she says.

Remember the adage "Underpromise and overdeliver," and give yourself some wiggle room on your delivery commitments. This was a lesson Adam Ginsberg learned when he had to keep his customers happy when the freight company he was using—the third largest in the United States at the time—went bankrupt and ceased operations with 50 of his tables en route to their destinations. While that was an unusual situation, you will still have to cope with situations that are beyond your control. "If you tell people one thing and you do something else, eBay buyers hold it against you with your feedback," Ginsberg says. "And who knows what can happen? The freight company might not show up for a week after you call them. Or there will be a snowstorm, and it will be delayed. All kinds of things can happen with shipping."

Without a doubt, shipping is a functional necessity, and it can be a disaster waiting to happen. But it can also be a marketing tool. Offer choices so your customers can select how fast they want to receive their merchandise and how much they want to pay. Consider offering free shipping on big items, Buy It Now items, or multiple purchases, or combine shipping on several small items.

If potential bidders send you e-mails asking how much shipping will cost for one of your auction items, have them send you their ZIP code, and then use the postage calculators at www.usps.com or www.ups.com (or whatever carrier you're considering using) to figure the exact cost. Another alternative is to say something in your auction description like "This item will be shipped from Tustin, CA, 92780, and it weighs 5 pounds, 4 ounces, with box and packing materials. To figure shipping costs to your ZIP code, visit www.usps.com or www.ups.com." That way, potential bidders can figure the shipping costs themselves and not have to send you an e-mail and wait for your reply.

Packing

Good packing is essential to protect your merchandise while it's in transit. Remember that your packages are going to be on a truck with other packages, they'll probably be loaded and unloaded several times, they'll likely experience bumps and vibrations, they may have other boxes stacked on top of them, and they may get dropped (or tossed around) repeatedly. All the "fragile" stickers in the world won't protect a carelessly packed shipment from damage. Your best line of defense against freight damage is to pack your items to travel safely. Heed these tips:

- Use only sturdy cartons that can be completely sealed. Corrugated boxes are usually best.
- Pack firmly, but don't overload the box. Cartons should not rattle or bulge.
- Maintain a padded space between your item and the wall of the box to absorb shocks.
- Each item should be wrapped individually in paper or cloth and separated from other items with sufficient cushioning to prevent damage from shock or vibration.
- Pack items in layers, placing the heaviest items on the bottom and the lightest on top.
- Do not pack hard or heavy items in the same box with fragile items.

- Seal each box completely with appropriate packaging tape. Don't use duct tape, electrical tape, cellophane tape, or masking tape on your packages. These tapes might be great for a variety of other functions, but they're not good for securing packages—they tend to peel off and/or deteriorate during transit. Do not use string; it can get caught in automated sorting equipment and damage both the equipment and your package. Paper over-wrap is discouraged for the same reason.

> **Smart Tip** Tip...
>
> Many package carriers (USPS, FedEx, and UPS, to name a few) provide packaging materials for certain service levels for free. The USPS, for example, provides free boxes for Express and Priority Mail shipments; however, it is against the law to use those boxes for any other purpose. Ask carriers what they provide and what restrictions apply.

- Label each carton with the name and address of both the shipper and the recipient. Number the boxes in the case of multicarton shipments (example: Box 1 of 2, Box 2 of 4, etc.).

- Include an inside label with complete shipper and recipient names and addresses in case anything happens to the outside label and it can't be read.

- Many shipping experts recommend using only new boxes, but eBay sellers routinely reuse boxes with satisfactory results. If you are reusing a box, be sure it's in good condition, and remove any old labels and shipment markings.

- If you are buying new merchandise from a manufacturer or wholesaler, consider having them pack your merchandise so it's ready for you to ship out rather than in bulk. You'll have to pay extra, but you'll save on in-house labor and supplies.

Choosing a Carrier

There is a wide range of differences in the pricing and service levels of various package and freight carriers, and it's a good idea to become familiar with them before making a decision on which carrier to use. Customers will view your choice of carrier and the service they provide as an extension of your operation, so it's important to use one that delivers a high level of customer service and reliability. Don't make your decision based on cost alone; as important as price is, the lowest price is not always the best value.

It's important to understand the difference between a package carrier and a common carrier. Package carriers (such as UPS, FedEx, and the USPS) handle smaller shipments with per-package weight limits typically ranging from 70 to 150 pounds. Many offer a choice of ground or air service. Common carriers are truck lines that handle large, heavy shipments that are too big for the package carriers.

When choosing a carrier, points to consider include:

- What are the size and weight limitations, and how does that compare with what you are shipping?
- What levels of service are available?
- Does the carrier offer online package tracking? How easy or difficult is it to use?
- Will the carrier make multiple delivery attempts without charging an extra fee?
- Does the carrier offer e-mail notification to let your customer know the package is on the way?
- Does the carrier deliver on Saturdays and, if so, is there an extra charge?
- How late will the carrier make pickups at your facility, and how does this blend with your work schedule?
- Does the carrier have a facility where your customers can pick up their package? (This is known as "hold for pickup.")

Tip...

Smart Tip

The post office will provide you with free lightweight plastic tubs that you can use to carry your smaller packages and envelopes—all you have to do is ask. Return the tubs when you no longer need them.

The Best Things in Life Are Free

Let everyone know that you'll take packing materials off their hands. Linda Parker says her husband's co-workers routinely save sturdy boxes, foam peanuts, and bubble wrap for her. "Packing materials are expensive, especially when you wrap a lot of glass like I do," she says. "So I appreciate my friends and my husband's associates keeping me stocked with this stuff."

Laurie Ayers gets large quantities of free bubble wrap from a local furniture store. "I have a friend who works there, and she gave me a heads-up on it," she says. "It's amazing what you can get for free when you ask. Companies that receive picture frames and other large fragile items get lots of packaging materials, and all they do is throw it away. So a few times a year, I go to my friend's store, fill up the back of my Jeep, and I'm good for months."

A great source of free shredded paper is your local post office. Your local postmaster may be willing to provide you with shredded nonsensitive returned mail to use as packing material. Another source of inexpensive paper filler is the end rolls of newsprint that are available from your local newspaper; often these are free or available for a nominal charge.

- Does the carrier offer return services to help you retrieve packages if necessary?
- Will the carrier provide delivery confirmation and, if so, is there an extra charge?
- Is the carrier financially stable?

Carrier selection is important not only for what you are shipping out but also for what you receive. If you are paying the freight on your incoming materials, you have the right to name the carrier. Beyond that, as a matter of good customer service, your suppliers should be willing to honor your carrier choice.

International Shipping

Many eBay sellers don't like to ship overseas because they don't understand the process or find it to be too much work. But if you take the time to learn how to do it—and for most countries, it's not complicated—you can increase your profits significantly.

Laurie Ayers says being willing to ship internationally gives her an edge over sellers who won't do it. "International people often don't have as many options, and if they're looking for something in particular, chances are they will bid higher," she says. "They pay the shipping, and the rates vary depending on the country. [Shipping to] some countries doesn't cost much more than shipping within the States, and to some the rates are ridiculous. I've had customers spend $40, $60, and more on shipping, but it was the only way they could get the item, so they were willing to pay."

The package and freight companies that deliver overseas (USPS, UPS, FedEx, etc.) have plenty of information to help you understand the procedures and paperwork necessary to ship to various international destinations. Contact the individual companies, or visit their Web sites for details.

Insurance

Beware!
Never just sign a delivery receipt for packages. Even though you'll get to know your regular driver, always count the packages and do a quick visual inspection for external signs of damage.

Insurance protects you and your customers by paying to replace or repair items that are damaged in transit. For high-end or very fragile merchandise, insist that your buyers pay for insurance for the full value of the goods. For low-end or very sturdy merchandise, you may allow buyers to make the choice of whether or not to buy insurance. But stress that if they reject insurance, your responsibility ends with shipping. Be sure you can prove that you shipped the

> ### Bright Idea
>
> Reusing old cartons for shipping? You can make them look new with mask-out paint, a colored spray paint that dries instantly and will accept your own labels and tape. This product is available through most shipping supply sources.

merchandise, either by using a carrier (such as UPS or FedEx) that will provide you with a shipper's receipt, or by using the USPS delivery confirmation service.

Some carriers automatically provide coverage for loss or damage up to $100 per shipment at no extra charge; others charge for the first dollar of insurance coverage. Don't bother to buy insurance for more than you can prove the item is worth; the carrier will only reimburse you for the actual value, not for the amount of insurance you purchased. Documents that are generally accepted as proof of value include a current bill of sale, an invoice, or a statement from a certified appraiser.

Even when you purchase insurance, it's important that your items be properly packed for transit. If damage occurs and the carrier determines that the shipment was not appropriately packed, your claim (or the buyer's claim, in most cases) will likely be denied.

Prompt Shipping Is the Law

The FTC's rules for mail and telephone order merchandise also apply to orders placed over the Internet. You must have a reasonable basis for stating that a product can be shipped within a certain time. If you have the item in your inventory, that's usually not going to be a problem. But if you are depending on drop-shippers, you should be sure they are reliable. When you use a drop-shipper, you as the seller are responsible for complying with the law.

If your auction doesn't clearly state a shipment period, you must ship within 30 days of receiving the order. If you can't, you must notify the customer of the delay, provide a revised shipment date, and explain his right to cancel and get a full and prompt refund. Complete details of these federal rules, including detailed instructions for delay notifications, can be found at www.ftc.gov.

Marketing

Marketing is something many people don't like to do, but it can be as creative and as much fun as putting up and monitoring your auctions—and it's essential to the success of any business. The basic principles you'll use in marketing your business when you sell on eBay are the same as when you sell through any other channel. The most important thing to keep in mind about marketing is this: It's not an expense; it's an investment in your business.

Keep these questions in mind as you form your marketing plan:

- Who are your potential customers?
- How many of them are there?
- Where are they located?
- Who are they buying from now?
- Can you offer them anything their current supplier is not providing?
- How do you compare with your competitors?
- What kind of image do you want your company to project?

Smart Tip

Before you try any marketing idea, take the time up front to figure out whom you're trying to reach and what you want to accomplish. Without a solid plan and sufficient research, you'll just waste your time and money.

The goal of your marketing plan should be to convey your existence and the quality of your service to prospective customers, ideally using a multifaceted approach. Chapter 10 in *Start-Up Basics* explains how to create a basic marketing plan.

Marketing Ideas that Work

Even though millions of people browse eBay every day, there's no guarantee that they're going to look at or bid on your auctions. That's why you need to be proactive in your efforts to get their attention.

Advertise

You may want to invest in advertising your auctions. This is an especially good idea when you have high-ticket items with substantial profit margins. Very few eBay sellers advertise their auctions outside eBay.

If you're going to go this route, choose a publication with a national circulation (such as *The Wall Street Journal*, *USA Today*, or *The New York Times*) and run a small classified or display ad in the appropriate section that describes what you're auctioning and includes the URL to locate the items on eBay.

The Element of Scarcity

One of the most powerful sales motivators is scarcity—that is, tapping into a bidder's fear that if he doesn't win this item right now, he'll never have a chance to acquire this item again. In your promotional materials—your listings, your own Web site, your About Me page on eBay, your advertisements—use this tool whenever possible.

Be creative. Don't just say "Due to a limited supply, we are allowing only five widgets per customer." That's been overdone, and most people recognize it for what it is. Try something like "Due to unusual weather conditions in the region where our suppliers are located, we don't know when we will get another shipment of these items at this price, so get yours now."

Cross-Promote

Each of your auction listings should also promote another auction listing and give the bidder a reason for checking out your other items. At the very least, suggest that the bidder take a look at your other items—the link eBay provides ("View seller's other items") makes it easy. To be more sophisticated, insert your own link using HTML, and make a specific

> **Bright Idea**
> If your storage area is smoke-free, mention that when writing your auction listing. That is often a big selling point for nonsmokers.

pitch. For example, "If you like this necklace, you'll love the earrings I'm selling, and I'll combine shipping if you win both auctions."

Keep an Eye on the Calendar

Make your auctions relative to the calendar. Tie your listings in to upcoming holidays or seasonal events. At ZBilliards, Adam Ginsberg says he changes the theme of his auctions monthly. For example, the theme for January is football and the Super Bowl, February is obviously Valentine's Day, he uses a basketball theme reflecting March Madness during that month, and so on. "We just like to change the look every month," he says.

Write Great Descriptions

We discussed the importance of good item descriptions in Chapter 5, but the issue cannot be stressed too strongly. With an online auction or Internet sale, you do not have the opportunity for face-to-face interaction where you can see your customer's expression, nor does your customer have the opportunity to actually see

> **Beware!**
> Even if everything you put in your auction description is true, if you leave out something important, your ad could be seen as misleading and subject to action by the FTC.

your merchandise. Write item descriptions that will work hard for you. Here's an excellent example: In a listing for a candy dish, an eBay seller described the dish in great detail, including measurements, color and design, and then added, "This dish holds a 13-ounce bag of Hershey's kisses." How much easier it was for a shopper to see that dish in her own home filled with chocolates!

Word-of-Mouth

Word-of-mouth is the most powerful form of marketing. Don't be shy about asking your family, friends, associates, and off-eBay customers to check out your auctions and visit your eBay store. You should also ask them to spread the word to their friends—if you're offering quality merchandise, they'll be happy to help.

Special Purchases

Special purchases can be a marketing tool. When you find a super deal on a great product, let your existing customers know what you've got, and tell them they need to buy now to take advantage of this special price.

Rules about Advertising

Online advertisements—and your eBay auctions are advertisements—are subject to the same rules that apply to other forms of advertising. In short, advertising must tell the truth and not mislead consumers, and claims must be substantiated.

One of the key missions of the FTC is to prevent deceptive and unfair acts or practices. According to the FTC, a representation, omission, or practice is deceptive if it is likely to mislead consumers and affect consumers' behavior or decisions about the product or service. An act or practice is unfair if the injury it causes or is likely to cause is substantial, not outweighed by other benefits, and not reasonably avoidable. Federal law prohibits unfair or deceptive advertising in any medium.

If you are selling goods you obtain from a manufacturer or distributor, ask for material to back up claims before you repeat what the manufacturer says about the product in your listing. If the manufacturer fails to provide the proof or gives you something that looks questionable, be very cautious about proceeding. Trust your instincts, and if the claims sound too good to be true, they probably are. And remember that all disclaimers and disclosures must be clear and conspicuous.

If your advertisements fail to comply with the law, you could face enforcement actions or civil lawsuits. That could mean orders to cease and desist, with fines up to $11,000 per violation; injunctions by federal district courts; and in some instances, refunds to consumers for actual damages in civil lawsuits.

Publicity and Public Relations

To gain the benefits of publicity and public relations, you must first understand what they are and why they're important to your business. A very simple way to explain publicity is that it is the process of getting yourself, your company, or your product mentioned in a print or broadcast story. You do this by suggesting to journalists—usually in the form of a news release, but you could also do it over the phone or via e-mail—that there is something about your organization that is newsworthy or otherwise of strong enough interest to be featured. You do not pay for this coverage, nor do you have any control over what journalists ultimately say in their coverage. This is in stark contrast to advertising, where you buy the space and control exactly what goes in it.

Public relations includes publicity, but it is a broader issue that encompasses such efforts as public image, investor relations, crisis communications, special events, and sponsorships, and other activities that have an influence on how the public perceives you and your company.

By virtue of its tremendous size and market, eBay as a company is routinely covered in the business media. That's good for all eBay sellers because it attracts new users, and therefore more potential customers for you.

But the publicity that will be of the most value to you is the publicity you generate yourself. When you do something that's newsworthy, issue a release to your local media outlets. If the business section of your local paper includes new business announcements, be sure yours gets in there. When you add a product line, expand your services, reach a certain sales goal, or hire new people, issue a news release.

When something happens on a national level that relates to what you do or the types of merchandise you sell, write up a media advisory with a local spin. Local reporters love to be able to interview someone in their own community. You can send a note (either fax or e-mail) to the local paper and radio and television stations repeating the news story and offering to answer additional questions.

When you see print or broadcast stories on people who are selling interesting or unusual items on eBay, those pieces are usually prompted by the eBay users, not eBay's corporate public relations department, says Kevin Pursglove, eBay's spokesperson. He says the mission of eBay's PR staff is to deal with corporate public relations, and they do not have the resources to help promote individual auctions or sellers. Also, sellers are likely to be more familiar with their specific media outlets, such as local and industry publications. "Generally, it's

Smart Tip

Tip...

When you see an ad or other marketing effort being repeated over time, it's a good sign that it's working, and you should consider using the same technique for your own company.

the seller who generates the media attention," he notes. "It's interesting how human psychology works here. A reporter [will often] be much more interested in covering a story about an item on eBay if that overture comes from the seller, and not from a paid PR person on the eBay payroll."

Trade Shows

Regardless of what type of items you sell on eBay, you may benefit from attending and possibly even exhibiting in trade shows. Shows provide a venue for you to find merchandise that you can sell on eBay, make contacts with wholesalers and other business product and service providers, learn more about running your business, and market your own products. Local trade shows can provide a tremendous amount of exposure at a very affordable cost and can be a great networking opportunity.

There are two types of shows—consumer (which focus on home, garden, and other consumer themes) and business-to-business (where exhibitors market their products and services to other companies).

"When you go to a show, you're tapping into an audience that is typically outside your network," says trade show consultant Allen Konopacki. "The other important thing is that the individuals who are going to shows are usually driven by a need. In fact, 76 percent of the people who go to a show are looking to make some kind of a decision on a purchase in the near future."

David Schultz exhibits in consumer trade shows targeted to expectant mothers and young families that are in the market for infants' and children's furniture, and expects to do more of that type of marketing and selling as he expands his product line. A show is an opportunity to let prospective customers see your merchandise on display so they'll feel more comfortable bidding on your auctions or shopping in your eBay store. Of course, if they buy at the show, all the better.

To find out about local shows in your area, call your local chamber of commerce or convention center and ask for a calendar. You can also check out *Trade Show Week Show Directory* (Reed Business Information), which should be available in your public library, or do an Internet search.

> **Tip...**
>
> ## Smart Tip
>
> Trade shows and conventions are valuable business tools, whether you're attending to shop and learn or exhibiting to get more business. For information on how to get more out of trade shows and to find show schedules, visit these trade show Web sites: Incomm Research Center, www.tradeshowresearch.com; Trade Show Central, www.tscentral.com; Trade Show News Network, www.tsnn.com; and Tradeshow Week Online, www.tradeshowweek.com.

When you have identified potential shows, contact the sponsor for details. Find out who will attend—show sponsors should be able to estimate the total number and give you demographics so you can tell if the attendees fit your target-market profile. Also ask if it's appropriate to make sales from your booth so you can plan your display and bring sufficient inventory.

Give as much thought to the setup of your booth as you would to an in-store display. Your exhibit does not need to be elaborate or expensive, but it does need to be professional and inviting. Avoid trying to cram so much into your booth that it looks cluttered. Your signage should focus first on the problems you solve for clients and then list your company name. Even though the show sponsors will probably provide

On with the Trade Show

A carnival-like atmosphere permeates many trade shows. Of course, you want everyone involved to enjoy themselves, but remember, this is a business occasion. Your booth is your store/office for the duration of the show, and it should be a place where you are proud to meet with customers. Establishing dress and conduct rules for your booth ahead of time will make your trade show experience much more rewarding. Abide by these rules:

- *No smoking, drinking, eating, or gum-chewing by booth staffers.* Too many people are offended by cigarette smoke, and most exhibit halls restrict smoking to designated areas anyway. While most shows provide refreshments, bringing food and beverages into the booth creates an unattractive mess. Who wants to talk to a sales rep whose mouth is full of Cheetos?
- *Dress appropriately.* Just because the show takes place at a resort doesn't mean you should wear shorts and a tank top. Standard business attire and comfortable shoes are your best bet.
- *Staff the booth properly.* Two people for every 10 feet of space is a good rule of thumb. The key is to make sure your booth is not overcrowded with your own people, or so understaffed that visitors can't get the assistance they need.
- *Take regular breaks.* Trade shows can be exhausting. Plan to allow everyone a few minutes away from the booth at scheduled intervals. Also allow time for personnel to see the entire show as early as possible; they'll gain a feel for the competition and pick up ideas for your next show.
- *Remain standing and talk to each other only when necessary.* Visitors may be reluctant to approach your booth if it appears your salespeople are just relaxing and having a great time chatting among themselves.

▲

one, do not put a table across the front of your exhibit space; that creates a visual and psychological barrier and will discourage visitors from coming in.

Don't leave your booth unattended during exhibit hours. First, it's a security risk— at a busy show, it would be easy for someone to walk off with valuable merchandise. But more important, you could miss a tremendous sales opportunity. Even if you're a one-person operation, find someone who can work the show with you so that you can take breaks during the day.

Consider some sort of giveaway item such as pens, mugs, or notepads imprinted with your company name. But, says Konopacki, do not display these items openly; that will only crowd your booth with "trade show tourists." Instead, store them discreetly out of sight, and present them individually as appropriate. You should also have a stock of brochures, business cards, and perhaps discount coupons.

To collect lead information for later follow-up, consider holding a drawing that people must register for, and make the registration form a lead-qualification tool that asks for information so you can follow up with a sales call later. When the show is over, immediately send a letter to all the qualified leads you collected, thanking them for visiting your booth and reminding them of the products and services you offer. Don't assume that they'll keep the information they picked up at the show; chances are, it will be lost in the pile of material they received from other exhibitors.

Chapter 12 in *Start-Up Basics* goes into greater detail on using this powerful promotional tool.

15

Staffing Your
Company

Plenty of eBay sellers make comfortable incomes as solo operators, handling everything themselves. They deliberately keep their companies as one-person operations because they don't want to deal with the headaches that growth can bring. They're happy that way and have no desire to do anything different. While there's nothing wrong with this strategy, if your goal is growth, you will reach a point where you must hire people. And even if your goal isn't growth, there may be times when you need help, so it's important to understand the basics of finding, hiring, and managing personnel.

You may find it difficult to turn over tasks to someone else, especially if you've never supervised or managed people before. There's little anyone else can tell you to make this leap easier; you just have to do it—and believe that it will be worth the effort. ZBilliards' Adam Ginsberg says he now has three to four full-time office people, plus his warehouse staff, which fluctuates. But he admits that one of the biggest mistakes he made as his business grew was trying to do too much himself and not hiring customer service staffers soon enough.

With this in mind, let's consider the process of adding staff to your operation. The first step is to decide exactly what you want someone to do and write a job description. The job description you write doesn't have to be as formal as one you might expect from a large corporation, but it needs to clearly outline the person's duties and responsibilities. It should also list any special skills or other required credentials, such as a valid driver's license and clean driving record for someone who is going to take packages to the post office and run other errands for you, or computer skills for administrative help.

Next, you need to establish a pay scale. This will depend on what you are hiring people to do, the skills needed, and the pay scales in your area. All the eBay sellers we talked to who had employees say they pay their staff competitively, based on their job descriptions and the market.

You should also have a job application form. You can get a basic form at most office supply stores, use the one provided in Chapter 6 in *Start-Up Basics*, or you can create your own. No matter which one you choose, have your attorney review the form you will be using for compliance with the most current employment laws.

Every prospective employee should fill out an application—even if it's someone you already know, and even if they've submitted a detailed resume. A resume is not a signed, sworn statement acknowledging that you can fire them if they lie; the application is. The application will also help you verify their resumes; compare the two and make sure the information is consistent.

Now you're ready to start looking for candidates.

Looking for Employees in All the Right Places

Picture the ideal candidate in your mind. Is this person likely to be unemployed and reading the classified ads? It's possible, but you will probably improve your chances for a successful hire if you're more creative in your search techniques than simply writing a "help wanted" ad.

Network with personal and professional associates to identify prospective employees—you never know who might know the perfect person for your company. Check with nearby colleges and perhaps even high schools for part-time help.

Smart Tip

Tip...

Consider how you can tie compensation to performance so workers have a clear incentive to do a great job.

Another option is to use a temporary help or employment agency. Many small businesses shy away from agencies because they feel like they can't afford the fee—but if the agency handles the advertising, initial screening, and background checks, their fee may be well worth paying.

Use caution if you decide to hire friends and relatives—many personal relationships have not been strong enough to survive an employee-employer situation. Small-business owners tell of nightmarish experiences when a friend or relative refused to accept direction or in other ways abused a personal relationship in the course of business. Jonathan Garriss, whose partner in their eBay business, Gotham City Online, is a friend, notes that small-business owners tend to hire people they know. "One of the challenges when you hire someone you know is that it's tough to separate business from friendship, and eventually the relationship changes," he says. He says it's critical to establish boundaries from the start. "Make sure both parties understand that this is a business relationship, and in the office you are boss and employee."

Evaluating Applicants

What kinds of people make good employees for a company that sells on eBay? It depends on what you want them to do. If you're hiring someone as a driver, that person should have a good driving record and know the city. If you're hiring someone to help with administrative tasks, they need to have computer know-how and be able to learn your operating system. If you're hiring someone to handle customer service, they need to know your products and policies, care about people, and be able to react quickly and calmly to surprises. What is really important is that the people you hire are committed to giving you their best effort during the time they're working so that your customers receive the best service.

Jonathan Garriss of Gotham City Online has about 20 employees, most of them full time. He says that everyone who works for him, from office staff to warehouse workers, is comfortable with technology and knows about clothing. "Everyone is using technology here," he says. "But they're not a bunch of techies. They know clothing, they know fashion, and they know their jobs. The way we have integrated technology makes their jobs easier."

When you actually begin the hiring process, don't be surprised if you're as nervous at the prospect of interviewing potential employees as they are about being interviewed. After all, they may need a job—but the future of your company is at stake.

It's a good idea to prepare your interview questions in advance. Develop open-ended questions that encourage the candidate to talk. In addition to knowing what they've done, you want to find out how they did it. Ask each candidate the same set of questions, and take notes as they respond so you can make an accurate assessment and comparison later.

When the interview is over, let the candidate know what to expect. Is it going to take you several weeks to interview other candidates, check references, and make a decision? Will you want the top candidates to return for a second interview? Will you call the candidates, or should they call you? This is not only a good business practice; it's also simple common courtesy.

Always check the former employers and personal references of your candidates. Though many companies are very restrictive as to what information they'll verify, you may be surprised at what you can find out. You should at least confirm that the applicant told the truth about dates and positions held. Personal references are likely to give you some additional insight into the general character and personality of the candidate; this will help you decide if they'll be a match for your culture and fit into your operation.

Be sure to document every step of the interview and reference-checking process. Even very small companies are finding themselves the targets of employment discrimination suits; good records are your best defense if it happens to you.

Once They're on Board

The hiring process is only the beginning of the challenge of having employees. The next thing you need to do is train them.

Many small businesses conduct their "training" just by throwing someone into the job, but that's not fair to the employee, and it's certainly not good for your business. If you think you can't afford to spend time on training, think again—can you afford not to adequately train your employees? Do you really want them interacting with your customers when you haven't told them how you want things done?

In an ideal world, employees could be hired already knowing everything they need to know. But this isn't an ideal world, and if you want the job done right, you have to teach your people how to do it.

Whether done in a formal classroom setting or on the job, effective training begins with a clear goal and a plan for reaching it. Training will fall into one of three major categories: orientation, which includes explaining company policies and procedures;

job skills, which focuses on how to do specific tasks; and ongoing development, which enhances the basic job skills and grooms employees for future challenges and opportunities. Heed the following tips; doing so will help maximize your training efforts:

- *Find out how people learn best.* Training employees is not a one-size-fits-all proposition. People absorb and process information differently, so your training method needs to be compatible with their individual preferences. Some people can read a manual, others prefer a verbal explanation, and still others need to see a demonstration. In a group training situation, your best strategy is to use a combination of methods; when you're working one-on-one, tailor your delivery to fit the needs of the person you're training. With some employees, figuring out

---

You Deserve a Break Today

No matter how much you enjoy your work, you need an occasional break from it. This is a particular challenge for solo operators, but it's critical. You need to be away from your operation occasionally, not only for vacations but also for business reasons, such as attending conferences and trade shows. Also, you need a plan in place in case of illness, an accident, or other emergencies.

Jonathan Garriss of Gotham City Online points out that as hard as he works, he knows how important it is to "take a little bit of time off and decompress." David Schultz of IEP Visions agrees. "There is no doubt about it. When we work hard, we overload ourselves. You have to take your days off."

If you're a one- or two-person operation, with proper planning you should be able to take a long weekend or just one or two days off without your customers even knowing you're gone. For longer periods away, you need to find someone you can trust who will run the business for you in your absence. With a staff to depend on, taking a vacation is easier—just be sure your people are well-trained and committed to maintaining your service levels when you aren't there.

Try these vacation-planning tips on for size:

○ *Plan ahead.* Schedule your vacation time far enough in advance that you can plan your workload around your time off. For example, you can stop listing auctions while you're gone.

○ *Build a backup network.* Look for people you trust who can handle work that can't wait while you're gone, such as orders from your eBay store or Web site.

○ *Notify your regular customers.* About two weeks before you leave, tell the customers with whom you communicate regularly that you'll be unavailable so they can place any upcoming orders before you go.

how they learn best can be a simple matter of asking them. Others may not know what their preferred learning style is. In those cases, experiment with various training styles and see what works best for the specific employee.

- *Use simulation and role-playing to train, practice, and reinforce.* One of the most effective training techniques is simulation, which involves showing an employee how to do something, and then allowing them to practice it in a safe, controlled environment.

- *Be a strong role model.* Don't expect more from your employees than you expect from yourself. You're a good role model when you do things the way they should be done all the time. Don't take shortcuts you don't want your employees to take, and don't behave in any way that you don't want them to behave. On the other hand, don't assume that simply doing things the right way is enough to teach others how to do things. Role-modeling is not a substitute for training—it reinforces training. If you only act as a role model but never train others to be one, employees aren't likely to get the message.

- *Look for training opportunities.* Once you get beyond basic orientation and job-skills training, you need to constantly be on the lookout for opportunities to enhance the skills and performance levels of your people.

- *Make it real.* Whenever possible, use real-life situations to train. For example, you might want to let a new customer service rep draft responses to bidder e-mails,

Cover Me

In most states, if you have three or more employees, you are required by law to carry workers' compensation insurance. This coverage pays medical expenses and replaces a portion of the employee's wages if he or she is injured on the job. Even if you have only one or two employees, you may want to consider obtaining this coverage to protect both them and yourself in the event of an accident.

Details and requirements vary by state; contact your state's insurance office or your own insurance agent for information so you can be sure you're in compliance. You'll also find more information in Chapter 7 of *Start-Up Basics*.

but you or another experienced worker should review them before they're sent. If you do this, be sure to avoid letting customers know they've become a training experience for employees.

- *Anticipate questions.* Don't assume employees know what to ask. In a new situation, people often don't understand enough to ask questions. Anticipate their questions, and answer them in advance.

- *Ask for feedback.* Just as your eBay customers let you know what they thought of their transaction with you, encourage employees to tell you how you're doing as a trainer. Explain that you'll evaluate their performance, so it's OK for them to tell you the truth; ask them what they thought of the training and your techniques, and use that information to improve your own skills.

Employee Benefits

The actual wages you pay may be only part of your employees' total compensation. While many very small companies do not offer a formal benefits program, more and more business owners have recognized that benefits—particularly in the area of insurance—are extremely important when it comes to attracting and retaining quality employees. Regardless of the overall employment situation, competition for good people is stiff almost everywhere.

Typical benefits packages include group insurance (your employees may pay all or a portion of their premiums), paid holidays, and vacations. You can build employee loyalty by seeking additional benefits that may be somewhat unusual—and they don't have to cost much. For example, if you're in a retail location, talk to other store owners in your shopping center to see if they're interested in providing reciprocal employee discounts. You'll not only provide your own employees with a benefit, but you may get some new customers out of the arrangement.

Gotham City Online offers health insurance and is working on developing a 401(k) plan. Jonathan Garriss says he is always looking for ways to enhance the company's benefits package. ZBilliards' Adam Ginsberg says his benefits package includes medical and dental insurance.

For more on employee benefits, policies, procedures, and other human resource issues, read Chapter 6 in *Start-Up Basics*.

Short-Term Solutions

Children's furniture seller David Schultz has two full-time customer service reps who stay consistently busy. But his need for help in the warehouse fluctuates. IEP Visions

▲

Bright Idea

Look for special, unexpected ways to reward your employees for a job well done. Take them to lunch, give them gift certificates or tickets for recreational events, or simply recognize them in front of other employees.

receives 12 to 15 containers from overseas each month, and additional labor is needed to help unload those trucks when they arrive. On other days, Schultz and his regular staff can handle the routine shipping and inventory tasks. So rather than hire full-time workers for a job that's not full time, Schultz uses a temporary labor service. Though his actual hourly rate is higher than it would be if these were his employees, the overall savings in both cash and efficiency makes it worth it to him.

You may also find that certain tasks can be handled by an independent contractor or consultant. Consider outsourcing work in the areas of accounting and record-keeping, special marketing projects, etc. If you have tasks you need help with but that don't fit the parameters of a regular part- or full-time position, look for non-traditional ways to get them done.

16

Tales from
the Trenches

By now you should know how to get started and have a good idea of what to do—and what not to do—when you're selling on eBay. But nothing teaches as well as the voice of experience. So we asked established eBay sellers to tell us what has contributed to their success and what they think causes companies that don't make it to fail. Here's what they said:

Consider Advice Carefully

As soon as you go into business for yourself, you'll be deluged with well-meaning advice. Jonathan Garriss of Gotham City Online says, "We got so much advice from people, and, unfortunately, three-fourths of it was wrong. What paid off for us was to take a common-sense approach. Ask yourself 'Does this make sense?' "

He says it's important to first understand what you're doing, and then you can evaluate how advice from someone else will fit into your operation. "If there is something you don't understand or that doesn't make sense to you, think twice," he recommends. He says you'll often get advice from people who are working through business models that are decades old, using techniques that may have been cutting-edge 20 years ago, but that just won't work today.

A Sustainable Plan

EBay is full of stories—and, in fact, we've told some of them in this book—of people who pick up something for pennies and sell it for hundreds of dollars on eBay. "Those are great isolated success stories," says Garriss. "But if you're looking to build a business based on buying things for $1 and selling them for $1,000, that is not a sustainable business model."

It's important, he says, to have realistic expectations. "People think eBay is like the great California Gold Rush," he says. "But it's work. You need to have knowledge of the marketplace and an understanding of what your business is going to be."

Consultant Paul Mladjenovic says one of the biggest mistakes new eBay sellers make is "thinking that they are going to make a fortune with one listing, when they should be doing multiple listings, tweaking, learning, analyzing, upgrading, modifying, and understanding their market as they go along."

Cindy Mayer agrees: "People think they can buy a really cheap product and make a lot of money with not a lot of work. It just doesn't happen that way."

Though he's been lucky on eBay, part-time eBay seller Buz Moran says, "I'm not trying to hit a homerun every time. I'm just trying to turn my dime into a dollar."

 Beware!
Walk before you run. "When you first start listing items, don't put up 100 auctions at once," says eBay seller Cindy Mayer. "Just do a couple until you are used to keeping track of things."

Keep the Cash Flowing

Don't worry if you take a loss on an item every now and then. Understand what happened (usually it's because you paid more than you should have), and keep going. You need to maintain a steady cash flow if you're going to be in a position to take advantage of opportunities when they arise, so keep buying and selling, buying and selling.

Don't Charge Until You Ship

If you have your own credit card merchant account, get a pre-authorization for the amount of the sale, but don't actually charge your customer's account until you have shipped the merchandise, advises Adam Ginsberg of ZBilliards. If something happens and you are unable to ship immediately, customers are inclined to be far more forgiving and understanding if you haven't charged them for the merchandise they haven't received. This was a lesson he learned when the Los Angeles Harbor strike meant he couldn't take possession of inventory that had already been sold. His customers weren't happy, but they understood—and they didn't feel like they'd paid for something they didn't have.

Get Rid of Items That Don't Sell

It happens to every retailer at one time or another: You invest in inventory you thought would sell, but it doesn't. So what do you do with it? If you bought it from a wholesaler with a return policy, consider taking advantage of that. But in most cases, you'll need to dump that unsold inventory in some way.

Some ideas from successful eBay sellers are:

- *Batch like items together, and sell them as a lot on eBay.* "Instead of selling the items one at a time, lump them together and sell them all at once," antiques seller Sue Rudolph advises. "I had some antique Christmas ornaments that I tried to sell singly a couple of years in a row, but the reserves weren't met. So I put them all together in a group, and they sold for more than the total of what I wanted for them individually."

- *For multiple items that are identical, drop the price, and list them in a Dutch auction.* "If something has been sitting in the warehouse for a long time, we'll drop the price down to something incredible and sell it in a Dutch auction," says children's furniture seller David Schultz of IEP Visions. "We had some cribs that had been in inventory for four or five months. We didn't have any matching pieces, like cradles or changing tables, to go with them. So they weren't selling very well. We put five at a time up on a Dutch auction starting at $40 each, and they sold very quickly."

- *Reduce your starting bid and relist.* It's a fact of life in retailing: Sometimes you have to sell things at a loss to turn your inventory. "My inventory is small enough that I know if something has been around and unsold long enough, it's about to start costing me," says Cindy Hale. "I'll sell those items at or below cost because I need my money back to buy more things." Rudolph agrees: "Sometimes you have to dump stuff. You might end up taking a loss, but at least you've gotten rid of it."

- *Hold a garage sale.* Moran says that once or twice a year he holds his own garage sale to clear out eBay inventory that isn't selling.

- *Give it to charity, and take a tax deduction.* Gotham City Online's consignment agreement allows the company to donate merchandise that doesn't sell to charities. Similarly, Laurie Ayers often buys from thrift stores, so when something doesn't sell, she donates back to the store where she bought it so that they can sell it again.

The Bottom Line

Is selling on eBay for you? Perhaps. Only you can make that call. For those who are cut out for this type of business, the bottom line is that eBay is a fun and potentially profitable place to do business, whether your goal is to generate occasional part-time income working by yourself from home or to build a substantial operation with commercial facilities and employees—or something in-between. So if this sounds like your cup of tea, decide what you're going to sell, get out your camera, write your description, and go!

Appendix
EBay Business Resources

They say you can never be too rich or too thin. While these could be argued, we believe "You can never have too many resources." Therefore, we present for your consideration a wealth of sources for you to check into, check out, and harness for your own personal information blitz.

These sources are tidbits, ideas to get you started on your research. They are by no means the only sources out there, and they should not be taken as the Ultimate Answer. We have done our research, but businesses—like customers—tend to move, change, fold, and expand. As we have repeatedly stressed, do your homework. Get out and start investigating.

Associations and Organizations

Auction & Marketing Institute, 10520 Barkley, #9, Overland Park, KS 66212, (913) 381-7653, fax: (913) 381-7660, www.auctionmarketing.org

National Mail Order Association LLC, 2807 Polk St. NE, Minneapolis, MN 55418-2954, (612) 788-1673, fax: (612) 788-1147, www.nmoa.org

Online Auction Users Association, P.O. Box 351192, Westminster, CO 80035-1192, www.auctionusers.org

The Auction Guild Inc. (TAG), P.O. Box 154, Fayette, NY 13065, (877) SAFETAG, www.theauctionguild.com

Auction Software and Support

Andale Inc., online auction management products and services, 300 Ferguson Dr., Mountain View, CA 94043, (866) 220-5099 or (650) 230-3000, fax: (650) 230-3090, www.andale.com

Auction Hawk, eBay auction management products, www.auctionhawk.com

AuctionHelper Inc., auction management tools for online auctions, 28720 Roadside Dr., #275, Agoura Hills, CA 91301, www.auctionhelper.com

Auction Patrol, forums, tools, directory, picture, and auction management, www.auctionpatrol.com

Auction Watch, online auction management products and services, 851 Traeger Ave., #100, San Bruno, CA 94066, (650) 808-5800, www.auctionwatch.com

Auction Wizard 2000, auction management software, www.auctionwizard2000.com

Auctionworks Inc., online auction software and services, 1117 Perimeter Center West, #500 E, Atlanta, GA 30338, (877) 668-2655, fax: (770) 392-3314, www.auctionworks.com

ChannelAdvisor Corp., auction management tools, 5001 Hospitality Ct., #100, Morrisville, NC 27560, (866) 264-8594, fax: (919) 388-9405, www.channeladvisor.com

FairMarket Inc., online auction management and promotion services, 500 Unicorn Park Dr., Woburn, MA 01801, (800) 531-7871, fax: (781) 935-7617, www.fairmarket.com

ManageAuctions.com, online auction management services, 418 Normany Dr., Norwood, MA 02062, www.manageauctions.com

MyAuctionMate, auction management software, www.myauctionmate.com

Pics Plus Image Hosting, image hosting, www.pics-plus.com

SpareDollar Inc., auction management services, www.sparedollar.com

Zoovy Inc., auction management and e-commerce software, (877) 966-8948, fax: (760) 944-6820, www.zoovy.com

Consultants and Other Experts

Allen Konopacki, Ph.D., trade show consultant, Incomm Research Center,1005 N. LaSalle Dr., #100, Chicago, IL 60610, (312) 642-9377, www.tradeshowresearch.com

Paul Mladjenovic, consultant and small-business specialist and teacher of classes on Internet auctions, Prosperity Network, P.O. Box 1883, Ft. Lee, NJ 07024, (201) 714-4953, www.mladjenovic.com and www.superauctionlinks.com

Chuck Norman, CPA, Partner, Ernst & Young, One Seagate, Toledo, OH 43604, 419-321-5470, www.ey.com

Internet Resources

Consumer Product Safety Commission, www.cpsc.gov

Federal Trade Commission, www.ftc.gov

Internet Auction List, www.internetauctionlist.com

Smart Shipping, a variety of shipping resources, including carriers, supplies, and services, www.smartshipping.com

Stamps.com, Internet postage, www.stamps.com

U.S. Business Advisor, www.business.gov

Payment Resources

Authorize.Net Corp., 915 S. 500 East, #200, American Fork, UT 84003, (801) 492-6450, fax: (801) 492-6489, www.authorizenet.com

C2it by Citibank, (800) 200-3881, www.c2it.com

CCNow, (877) 226-6977, www.ccnow.com

E-Gold, (321) 956-1200, fax: (321) 951-0790, www.e-gold.com

Escrow.com, 1221 E. Dyer Rd., #225, Santa Ana, CA 92705, (714) 751-6290, fax: (714) 384-3412, www.escrow.com

Glo-Bill, 1255 Treat Blvd., 3rd Fl., Walnut Creek, CA 94597, (888) 746-4217, fax: (925) 687-9920, www.globill-systems.com

Internet Billing Co. Ltd., 2200 SW 10th St., Deerfield Beach, FL 33442, (888) 371-7800, fax: (954) 363-4407, www.ibill.com

Paying Fast, www.payingfast.com

PayPal, www.paypal.com

PaySystems.com Inc., 575 Madison Ave., 10th Fl., New York, NY 10022, (514) 227-6868, fax: (514) 227-6838, www.paysystems.com

Western Union BidPay, BidPay.com Inc., P.O. Box 850, Bridgeton, MO 63044, www.bidpay.com

WorldPay Inc., 21525 Ridgetop Cir., #175, Sterling, VA 20166, (703) 444-0260, fax: (703) 430-6795, www.worldpay.com

Publications

EBay for Dummies, Marsha Collier, Hungry Minds

Starting an eBay Business for Dummies, Marsha Collier, Hungry Minds

Starting Your Online Auction Business, Dennis L. Prince, Prima Tech

Shipping Companies

Airborne Express, www.airborne.com

FedEx, www.fedex.com

United Parcel Service (UPS), www.ups.com

United States Postal Service (USPS), www.usps.com

Successful eBay Sellers

Laurie Ayers, Granville, MI, (616) 249-0922, www.laurieayers.com, *eBay user ID:* ourpreciouskids

Busy Moms Recipes, Charlene Davis, Oviedo, FL, www.busymomsrecipes.com and www.cdavisfreelance.com, *eBay user ID:* theditzydog, *Elance user ID:* cdavisadm

Cindy's Collectibles, Cindy Mayer, e-mail: wjmayer@adelphia.com, *eBay user ID:* jocin3

Gotham City Online, Jonathan Garriss, 390 Broadway, New York, NY 10013, (201) 330-9093, www.gothamcityonline.com, *eBay user ID:* gothamcityonline

IEP Visions, David Schultz, 7101 Presidents Dr., #300, Orlando, FL 32809, (407) 859-8448, fax: (407) 859-8269, www.iepvisions.com, *eBay user ID:* iepvisions

Gary and Susan Marler, Selma, NC, (919) 965-0783, Gary's e-mail: wizard5482@bellsouth.net, Susan's e-mail: smarler514@bellsouth.net, *Gary's eBay user ID:* wizard5482, *Susan's eBay user ID:* ozfreak2

Buz Moran, Long Beach, CA, e-mail: jewel777@worldnet.att.net, *eBay user ID:* chubbychums

Sweet Sue's Antiques and Appraisals, Sue Rudolph, Winter Park, FL, e-mail: suru@worldnet.att.net, *eBay user ID:* suru2

The Walker Avenue Attic, Cindy Hale-Stapp, e-mail: cindyhale@hotmail.com, *eBay user ID:* cindyhale

ZBilliards, Adam Ginsberg, Los Angeles, CA, (877) ZBilliards or (310) 826-5276, www.zbilliards.com, *eBay user ID:* zbilliards

Glossary

About Me: an eBay page that tells other users about you.

Acquiring bank: in online payment processing, this is the bank that provides Internet merchant accounts.

Ad format listings: advertisements for products and services on eBay, as opposed to auctions.

Add-on selling: encouraging customers to buy additional, related items; also referred to as suggestive selling and companion selling.

Announcements Board: a special online bulletin board where eBay posts timely information and updates; regular eBay users should check this board daily.

Authorization: the process of verifying that a customer's credit card is active and that the customer has sufficient available credit to complete the transaction; for online payments, the authorization process also verifies the customer's billing information.

Auto sig: an automatic signature attached to your outgoing e-mail.

Bid cancellation: the cancellation of a bid by a buyer or seller.

Bid increment: the amount by which a bid is increased each time the current bid is outdone.

Bid retraction: the withdrawal of a bid; bid retractions are rarely allowed on eBay.

Bid shielding: using secondary user IDs or other eBay members to temporarily raise bidding to extremely high levels to protect the low bid level of another bidder; when bid shielding, the high bidder retracts the bid just before the auction closes.

Bidder search: a search for all the items on which a particular user has placed bids.

Bidding: the act of placing a bid on an auction item.

Bill of lading (BOL): the mandatory paperwork necessary when shipping by common carrier that includes all the details needed to process and bill the shipment.

C.O.D. (cash on delivery): payment at the time the merchandise is delivered or picked up by the customer.

Card not present: a term used by credit card companies to describe a transaction in which the seller has not seen the actual credit card; typically, this applies to Internet and mail order sales.

Completed search: a search of eBay auctions that have ended.

Customer issuing bank: a financial institution that provides a customer with a credit card or other payment instrument.

Cybercrime: crime related to technology, computers, and the Internet.

Dimensional weight: a standard formula used in the freight industry that considers a package's density when determining charges; charges are based on the actual weight or the dimensional weight, whichever is greater.

Discount: the amount by which a price is reduced to create an incentive for various consumer behaviors, such as to increase sales or encourage early payment.

Domain name: the textual name assigned to a host on the Internet.

Dutch auction: when a seller has two or more identical items offered in the same auction; also known as a multiple item auction.

Dutch avoidance: avoiding posting a Dutch auction by listing a single item and offering additional items for sale in the item description; this is a violation of eBay policy.

EBay Live auctions: a way to bid real-time at offline auctions through eBay.

Featured auction: a marketing service provided by eBay that gives auctions extra exposure in the "Featured" sections at the top of listings pages.

Feedback: comments made by one user about another regarding the trading experience between the two.

Final value: the final bid on an auction; the amount for which the item sells.

Final-value fee: the percentage of the final value that is paid by the seller to eBay as part of the listing fees.

Foot traffic: in retailing, the people walking by or in a store.

Gift services: an eBay service that allows you to feature your item as a gift and let buyers know that you offer services such as gift wrapping, cards, and shipping directly to the recipient.

Gondola: a type of display unit typically used in retail stores, usually a bank of free-standing shelves open on all sides; its primary function is to display goods and provide space for backup stock.

Hot item: a designation that appears in search results given to nonreserve items that have received more than 30 bids; hot items are symbolized by a burning-match icon.

HTML: stands for Hypertext Markup Language, a simple language used to create Web pages; this language can be used to enhance eBay listings.

Indefinite suspension: the suspension of a user's eBay privileges for more than 60 days, with no definite reinstatement date.

Insertion fee: the nonrefundable fee charged by eBay to post a listing; insertion fees vary by type of listing.

Internet merchant account: a special account with an acquiring bank that allows a merchant to accept credit cards over the Internet.

Internet service provider (ISP): any company that provides users with access to the Internet.

Item lookup: a method for searching for an item on eBay when you know the item number.

Marking guns: devices used to affix prices or bar codes to retail merchandise.

Markup: the amount by which the wholesale price of an item is increased to reach the retail price.

Merge: combining several eBay user IDs (including feedback scores and comments) into one.

Minimum bid: the lowest amount that can be entered as a bid for a specific auction.

Mint: a subjective term used to describe an item that is in perfect condition.

Multiple item auction: see *Dutch auction*.

New item: items listed within the preceding 24 hours are considered new and are automatically marked with a rising sun icon, which is removed when the listing is more than 24 hours old.

Nonpaying bidder: a bidder who wins an auction but does not pay for the item; eBay has strict policies for dealing with nonpaying bidders.

Opening value: another term for starting price or minimum bid.

Outbid: a bidder is outbid when another bidder has placed a higher maximum bid than theirs.

Outsource: hiring outside firms to provide products and services traditionally handled within a company.

Password: a data string used to verify the identity of a user.

Payment gateway: a service that provides connectivity among merchants, customers, and financial networks to process and authorize payments.

Piracy: the act of illegally copying software, music, or movies that are protected by copyright.

PowerSeller: an eBay designation for experienced, reputable eBay sellers who consistently sell a significant volume of items, maintain a 98 percent positive feedback rating, and provide a high level of service; PowerSellers are marked with icons next to their user IDs.

Private auction: a type of eBay auction where the bidders' e-mail addresses are not disclosed on the auction page or the bid history page.

Processor: a large data center that processes credit card transactions.

Proxy bidding: a service that allows you to enter the maximum amount you're willing to pay for an item; the eBay system automatically places bids on your behalf, increasing your bid as necessary by the standard increments to maintain your high-bid position.

Reserve price: a hidden minimum amount the seller is willing to accept for an item listed for auction.

Reserve price auction: in a reserve price auction, buyers are not shown the reserve price, and sellers are not obligated to sell if the reserve price is not met.

RMA: return merchandise authorization; usually a code number issued by a seller who agrees to accept a return.

SafeHarbor: the protective arm of eBay that monitors possible misuse of the eBay system and keeps the eBay community safe.

Shades icon: an icon that looks like a pair of sunglasses after a user ID that tells you the eBay member is either new or has changed their user ID within the past 30 days.

Shill bidding: the deliberate placing of bids to artificially raise the price of an item; shill bidding is not allowed on eBay and is illegal in many jurisdictions.

Shrinkage: a term used to describe losses when inventory is reduced by theft (either internally or externally) or errors.

Signposts: listings that are primarily meant to direct a user to a seller's store or other listings; signposts are not allowed on eBay.

Sniping: placing a bid in the closing minutes or seconds of an auction.

Spam: unsolicited commercial e-mail.

Starting price: the price at which bidding on your auction begins; also, the lowest price you are willing to accept unless you have specified a reserve price.

Supplier: a company that sells goods and services to other companies.

Trademark: any word, name, symbol or device, or any combination, used or intended to be used in commerce to identify and distinguish the goods of one manufacturer or seller from goods manufactured or sold by others, and to indicate the source of the goods.

Turbo Lister: an eBay service that allows sellers to create and upload bulk auction listings instead of manually entering information for each auction.

User ID: an eBay nickname or screen name chosen by the user.

Vendor: another term for supplier.

Index

Introduction

So you have made the decision to start your own business. Congratulations! You are joining the ranks of entrepreneurs and business leaders who are the reason our great country has been able to flourish as a business giant among the countries of the world. While all business owners certainly suffer setbacks as they drive their businesses toward success, on September 11, 2001, the business world, and the rest of the world, was turned upside down for a while.

Terrorists may have destroyed the Twin Towers in New York City and parts of the Pentagon near Washington, DC, but Americans—both business leaders and ordinary citizens—have responded with a renewed sense of purpose. A purpose that will ultimately depend on business leaders to become a beacon of hope in a sometimes dark and gloomy world.

As America began almost immediately to rebuild, business owners were responding and answering the call. They kept the economy moving forward at a time when our nation was relying on them to do so. And they did it successfully. You can, too!

You can join the ranks of American business owners and leaders who have been making this country a shining example to the rest of the world. But as with any successful journey, it begins with a plan. A carefully crafted plan. A *business plan*!

Each chapter in this book is devoted to analyzing, explaining, and, wherever and whenever possible, making entertaining, an important concept relating to business plans. The chapter topics range from why you even need a plan to what to do with it when you're finished. You'll learn techniques for figuring your break-even ratio and tips for approaching potential investors. You'll hear stories about the business plans of famous entrepreneurs and even learn about a few entrepreneurs who admit that they don't write plans—willingly, at least.

Along the way, you'll find sprinkled definitions of important terms, contact information for useful resources, warnings of especially common or serious mistakes, and pointers to steer you in the right direction. When you've finished reading the book, you'll be prepared to write a sound, comprehensive, convincing plan for almost any business, whether it's a brand-new start-up or an existing company. More important, however, you'll be the owner of a thoroughly prepared mind and need just the slightest nod from good fortune to proceed.

Following is a chapter-by-chapter summary of the book. The chapters are intended to be read in sequence, with exercises, worksheets, and samples to be studied, completed, and examined along the way. If after finishing you need more help with a particular section, the chapters can be reviewed as self-contained tutorials on their particular topics.

Chapter 1: Business Plan Basics

This chapter shows that there are many compelling answers to the question, Why write a business plan? It explores the basic definition of a business plan and when and why to write one. It provides detailed information on sources of capital and techniques for using your plan to raise money. It also describes using a plan as a tool for marketing your company to prospective partners, suppliers, customers, and even employees.

Chapter 2: Money Hunt

Writing a business plan is an activity closely tied to the idea of raising money for a start-up business. This chapter examines sources of funding and explains how business plans can be used to help entrepreneurs obtain financing from the most commonly used sources.

Chapter 3: The Big Picture

One of the most important purposes of a business plan is to evaluate a business proposition's chances for success. This chapter shows how to use a plan to see if a new venture is likely to achieve the desired results.

Chapter 4: Set Your Course

No two plans are the same, but they all follow similar routes to creation. This chapter tells how to navigate the major steps, including determining your personal goals and objectives and how they figure in planning. It also provides a first, brief look at the major plan elements: Executive Summary, Management, Product or Service, Marketing, Operations, and Financial Data, along with brief explanations of each.

Chapter 5: Match Game

You're unique and, in all likelihood, so is your plan. Plans differ among industries, for one thing, and they also have different purposes. You want to pick the general type of plan that fits your needs and your company. This chapter explains how to do that, as well as presents descriptions of the major types of plans, such as working plans, miniplans, and presentations.

Chapter 6: Sum It Up

The executive summary is the most important part of your plan. This chapter tells you why, and details exactly what should go into a well-conceived summary.

Chapter 7: Team Work

The section of your business plan where you describe your management team is likely to be one of the first readers turn to. You'll need to explain what each member of your team does, how you plan to grow it if necessary, and who your advisors are. This chapter explains the techniques and underlying import of all these tasks of the management section.

Chapter 8: Announcing...

Most entrepreneurs really enjoy describing the product or services that is their business's reason for being. This chapter tells how to channel that enthusiasm into answering the questions investors and other plan readers most often ask.

Chapter 9: Field Notes

Every business plan has to make the industry in which it will operate crystal clear. In this section you'll also describe the state of your industry using market research, trend analysis, and competitive factors to explain why you picked this industry; whether it's growing or shrinking; and what makes you better.

Chapter 10: Marketing Smarts

No matter how great your product or services are, if you don't know how to persuade someone to buy them, and show that you know it in your business plan, your plan will get short shrift. This primer in marketing strategy will tell how to employ the four Ps of traditional marketing as well as prepare a follow-up marketing plan for the next generation of products.

Chapter 11: The Works

Operations is another area few entrepreneurs have trouble mustering enthusiasm for. As usual, however, the entrepreneurial enthusiasm has to be directed at the right targets if the plan is to achieve maximum impact on its readers. This chapter tells how to write operations sections for manufacturers, service firms, and retailers, with special considerations for each.

Chapter 12: State Your Case

The most intimidating part of a business plan for many entrepreneurs is the required financial statements, including historical and projected balance sheets, income statements, and cash flow statements. This chapter dispels fears by clearly presenting explanations of the major financial statements and analytical ratios, along with instructions on how to prepare them and common pitfalls.

Chapter 13: Extra, Extra

Many plans have important information that doesn't fit into the major sections. This chapter tells you what to consider for a plan's appendix, including employee resumes, product samples, press clippings, and the like.

Chapter 14: Looking Good

Good presentation can make a good plan even better. You need to pick the proper stationery, printing, and design for your plan. You need to make sure that you use charts, graphs, and tables when appropriate, without overdoing it. This chapter provides straightforward tips for doing that, along with hints on multimedia presentations and other elements of a plan package such as cover sheets and cover letters.

Chapter 15: Help Line

There is as much information and assistance available on business plan writing as any entrepreneur could hope for. This chapter describes some of it, including software for writing business plans, books and how-to manuals, Web sites, trade groups and associations, business plan consultants, and even business plan competitions.

Chapter 16: The Internet and Your Planning Efforts

The Internet has leveled the playing field for business owners in the new millennium. In the old days, it was difficult or even impossible to find business information that would help your business succeed. Not any longer, because the Internet has become a wealth of information that is there for the picking. Learn how you can take advantage of the Internet to help your business succeed.

Appendices: Sample Business Plans

Here you will find sample business plans for five very different types of businesses. Everything from A to Z can be found in these plans, which can be used in part or in whole as models for your own business plan.

The Government Listings appendix provides contact information for Small Business Development Centers, Small Business Administration district offices, and state economic development departments across the country.

Scattered throughout the book you'll find various tip boxes. Each will provide useful information of a different type.

PLAN OF ACTION

Here we direct you to sources for more information and guidance.

PLAN PITFALL

This box warns you of common errors made by plan writers.

FACT OR FICTION?

Get straight answers to common business plan questions.

PLAN POINTER

This box offers advice on ways to improve your plan.

BUZZWORD

This box offers brief definitions of terms you'll run into in the process of writing your plan.

Available at all fine bookstores and online booksellers.
www.entrepreneurpress.com.